CABINET OFFICE
(MANAGEMENT AND PER*
CIVIL SERVICE COLLEGE

Effective Assignment Skills and Strategies

A Guide for Management Services Staff, Line Managers and Others

Alan Ruston
Ronald Ram

London
Her Majesty's Stationery Office

© *Crown copyright 1987*
First published 1987
Second Impression 1987
ISBN 0 11 430015 1

CONTENTS

	Page
INTRODUCTION	7

CHAPTER I: CHARACTERISTICS OF ASSIGNMENT WORK

1	Changing themes	9
2	The line manager's contribution	11
3	The specialist's contribution	12
4	Types of assignment	15
5	Assignment management	15

CHAPTER II: THE ASSIGNMENT OVERVIEW: BRINGING ABOUT CHANGE

1	What to plan for, and why	19
2	Bringing about change	20
3	The completion plan; achieving overall control	24

CHAPTER III: GETTING STARTED

1	Basic issues to be resolved	29
2	Entry	29
3	Contract	32

CHAPTER IV: ANALYSIS AND DIAGNOSIS

1	The need for a logical approach	35
2	Data collection and evaluation	37
3	Analysis	40
4	Diagnosis	43

CHAPTER V: USEFUL TECHNIQUES

1	Interviewing: basic understanding required	45
2	The professional interview	47
3	Using statistical techniques effectively	49
4	Statistical analysis	50
5	Work measurement	52
6	Costing of activities	52
7	Costing of proposals	54
8	Forms design	54
9	Operational research	55
10	Charting the work	55
11	Creative thinking	56

CHAPTER VI: FORMULATING THE PROPOSALS AND SEEKING AGREEMENT

1	The heart of the assignment	59
2	Formulating the proposals	59
3	Seeking agreement: the basic approach	61
4	Clinching an agreement	62

CHAPTER VII: COMMUNICATING THE FINDINGS

1	Purpose	65
2	The written report	65
3	The verbal report	68

CHAPTER VIII: IMPLEMENTATION

1	The importance of effective implementation	71
2	Responsibility for implementation	71
3	Planning implementation	72
4	Training	73
5	Withdrawal of the assignment officer	74

CHAPTER IX: APPLYING INFORMATION TECHNOLOGY

1	The main issues	75
2	Dimensions of importance in promoting the best use of information technology	77
3	Dimension I: Impact on how work is done	78
4	Dimension II: Availability and cost of equipment	79

5	Dimension III: Impact on management operations and structures	79
6	Dimension IV: Obstacles to acceptance of change	80
7	The importance of planning and appraisal in implementing projects	81

CHAPTER X: IMPROVING THE USE OF RESOURCES

1	Meeting the changing needs of management	83
2	The management services contribution	84
3	Important techniques	87

GLOSSARY 89

INDEX 93

INTRODUCTION

The theme of this book is not original, because the first official publication on the subject, *The Practice of O&M*, was issued in 1954. Many changes in the needs of line managers and the nature of assignment work have occurred since then. First, enormous technical improvements in the application of computers, increasingly linked with the means of communication, have affected the way in which work is completed and carried out. Secondly, there have been important changes in management style and in attitudes to the conduct of assignment work. Thirdly, the range of skills available to and required by assignment staff has increased. The number of separately identified disciplines has also grown, and the overall application of their services become more complex. For these reasons the general impact and impression presented by *The Practice of O&M* has become outdated. It is because of the need to re-express the original theme in contemporary terms, that this book has been written.

The thinking on which this book is based is drawn from a number of sources. Experience of teaching assignment staff at the Civil Service College is a prime one. Another is the general experience of College staff which is extensive, practical, and reflects the best of both public and private sector practice. Knowledge of related developments occurring in the Civil Service and elsewhere has also influenced the contents. A number of people, including practising management services staff and students on courses, have contributed ideas and played a part in the preparation of the text. To them thanks are expressed for the valuable assistance provided. In particular we would like to acknowledge the benefit we have derived from discussions with colleagues in the Management and Efficiency Division of the Cabinet Office (MPO).

The main aim is the same as in *The Practice of O&M*, namely to give advice on how to complete an assignment. This aspect is crucially important, for it is the core on which everything else depends. Failure to conduct work in a professional way can significantly diminish the ability to produce material improvements capable of implementation. A great deal of emphasis is therefore given to how assignments are planned and organised; and to the use of conceptual and analytical disciplines. This book is not designed to be a comprehensive manual, for information about particular techniques and subjects is available from a variety of sources including College course material.

The book's structure is based on the principal stages involved in the completion of an assignment. Chapters I and II are concerned with setting the scene and the more general issues that are of importance. Chapters III to VIII are devoted to outlines of practical advice and concepts relevant to each phase. The last two chapters address aspects that have become important since *The Practice of O&M* was written.

The book can be used in a number of ways. It can augment teaching of skills and techniques; indeed it provides an essential background to such teaching. It can profitably be read in conjunction with College handouts and other training material which supply detailed information on particular techniques. In contexts unrelated to the teaching environment at the Civil Service College the book offers a general introduction to assignment work. Practitioners can also dip into it for advice while working on an assignment.

The themes discussed should appeal to several types of audience. The book is a basic guide for new practitioners but it is hoped that it will also be of assistance to experienced staff interested in the changing nature of assignment work. Additionally it is expected to be an aid to line managers as they try to improve further the effective use of resources; it provides them with guidance on how to use, and maintain successful working relationships with, management services personnel. The management services disciplines do not have a prerogative on the use of the assignment method and the principles outlined are of use to anyone whose work is assignment based. People who work in organisations outside the British Civil Service, both in the United Kingdom and abroad, should find the book relevant to their needs, for many of the developments and changes discussed are not confined to the British Civil Service. No specific references to current Civil Service initiatives are made, although they have been fully taken into account. This is intentional so that the book can provide for longer-term needs, and be of value to a wide audience.

CHAPTER I: CHARACTERISTICS OF ASSIGNMENT WORK

1 Changing themes

It is now over 30 years since the management services divisions of Her Majesty's Treasury compiled the original version of *The Practice of O&M*. The objective of that initiative was to support the early development of disciplines to examine efficiency and effectiveness. The book reflected the major emphasis of the day, which was to secure improvement in procedures and work organisation at relatively junior levels. Over the intervening years several new and important developments have affected how work is done and attitudes to work, which in turn, are causing changes of emphasis in assignment work.

The growth of information technology has had a profound impact. The invention of mainframe machines made it possible to mechanise large-scale routine administrative tasks. The more recent appearance of microcomputers and related office technology is likely to have an impact of equal, or greater, dimensions, although its character will be different. The latest innovations encourage user independence and more extensive exploitation of computer potential, characteristics which fit well with the greater individual responsibility now being given to managers in the Civil Service.

Management's views about the use of resources have altered because of increased pressure to obtain better value from them. In this context three objectives, often interconnected, have come to the fore. One is the drive to reduce costs by careful budgeting and economy. Reductions, or better use, of capital, time, space and people frequently result in worthwhile savings. Manpower is not necessarily the most significant element. All expenditures need to be examined to identify where key savings can be made. The second places increased emphasis on the identification of clear, realistic objectives, which can promote improved levels of service and secure large savings through refinement of organisation structures. The third development is the introduction of major changes in management practice. Management accountability in the Civil Service has often been dispersed through the operating structure, but there has been a trend for some years to identify a clearer responsibility for the use of resources in key management posts, whether concerned with policy formulation or application. This pattern of working is now being introduced progressively to promote greater management efficiency.

A number of factors have led to more attention being paid to how change in working practices is achieved. Demands for greater effectiveness in all types of work, and the seemingly inexorable acceleration in the rate of technological innovation, increase the rate of change and make it essential to plan for its achievement. Developments in social attitudes have prompted less authoritarian and mechanistic approaches to both the content of work and to the introduction of new ways of working. People now question change and are concerned to be informed about its justification and impact. Failure to give sufficient attention to how change is secured can lead to the rejection or delayed and incomplete introduction of necessary new ways of working. To gain acceptance of change is a challenge, and involves hard work for all those involved, including people affected directly, line management, staff-side representatives and management services staff.

There have also been developments in the disciplines that comprise management services. Their range and sophistication has increased considerably. Operational Research, Statistics and Economics disciplines have all come to be applied to administrative activity in an organised way, and information technology has become more significant as the quantity and scope of computer applications has grown.

All the matters discussed above raise issues relevant to management services staff, eg organisational implications, design of related systems, support in monitoring, and advice on problems. The most important implications for assignment staff are noted here briefly, and will be discussed in more detail at appropriate points in the text.

Some of the most striking changes in assignment work have been prompted by the need to make better use of resources. The increased emphasis on examination of the necessity for work, on the justification of proposals in cost terms, and on assignment effectiveness are noteworthy examples of this pressure. More frequent requests to management services for assistance should result from greater management interest and involvement in efficiency and effectiveness issues. Management is more likely to place emphasis on the solution of general rather than specific problems, eg requests to help improve efficient management of an area of responsibility rather than to perfect a single procedure or operation. The range of skills and techniques used by assignment staff are becoming more extensive. Planning for change is becoming a vital component part of assignment work. This requires clarity and flexibility in the pursuit of objectives, effort and time in communicating with staff, care in the selection and testing of proposals, and above all, sensitivity to matters that might cause acceptance problems. Because of the drive to secure all-round increases in efficiency and effectiveness there is a greater emphasis on team working and shared assignments, involving staff in O&M, Staff Inspection, Operational Research, Internal Audit and other specialist disciplines as necessary. Finally, tighter discipline in project control is being developed, which should result in assignments being conducted with increased efficiency and effectiveness.

2 The line manager's contribution

The line manager is someone whose management responsibilities are directly concerned with the fulfilment of a department's main functions, and is usually the client of the assignment officer. The exact definition of 'client' and 'line manager' can vary however, depending on circumstances.* Developments in management accountability are causing line managers' involvement with efficiency matters to be reinforced at all levels, although in different ways, according to the nature of the responsibility held. Senior line managers are becoming more formally accountable for planning, controlling and monitoring departmental activities, and are interested to see that effective arrangements exist for the implementation of these responsibilities. Line managers primarily concerned with the achievement of specific tasks will have more clearly defined accountabilities and greater freedom to meet them within a stated overall framework. They are likely to have a lively interest in efficiency issues which affect their responsibilities.

It has already been stated that changes in the structure of man-

---

* The glossary at the end of the book provides definitions which clarify the meaning of these and other important terms and words used in the text.

agement accountability will lead to new emphases in assignment activity, and these will include closer working with line management than has often been the case. Whatever changes occur line managers will always bear the ultimate responsibility for the implementation of proposals, and the role of the specialist as adviser will continue to be important in its own right. Closer working between line management and management services personnel should promote better mutual understanding of the role played by each. It is advantageous if line managers are educated to make appropriate use of external reviews of the efficiency and effectiveness of their organisation, its methods of working, and how best to secure and evaluate the advice they receive.

Line managers at all levels are doing more themselves to improve efficiency within their areas of responsibility, through their own application of information technology. Such initiatives pose possible problems for the interrelationship between line managers and management services advisers. It is particularly important that line managers discriminate between what can be done usefully by themselves and when outside help is desirable. It is also important that their own efforts are compatible with wider organisational strategies.

3 The specialist's contribution

The involvement of specialists is justified solely by the value of the help given to the improvement of management performance. They are able to deploy professional qualities and attributes, using their training, experience and judgement, to resolve problems associated with running the administrative machine. But their main value stems from the uniqueness of their situation. They can bring a freshness of approach and an independence of view to a problem, which helps them to provide balanced and unbiased advice to management. The privilege attached to such a position has to be exercised with responsibility, and they need to recognise that some of the best suggestions can come from within the organisation being investigated. Assignment officers do not have a monopoly of ideas.

Good training of assignment staff is a necessary pre-requisite to successful management services practice. One requirement is to obtain understanding and competence in applying specific techniques. Another is acquiring the overall ability to work competently at an assignment, which is the most basic and difficult to learn.

Even though understanding the theory and practice of work methods and organisation, and of having a thorough knowledge of associated techniques is important, it is insufficient in itself. Judgement is also required, because problems which arise during an assignment are rarely resolved by reference to predetermined principles. Judgement is particularly significant in knowing how to approach people; how to obtain, record and verify information; how to classify it, build it up, and finally, how to test and evaluate conclusions. The specialist above all needs to be aware that his or her services can only produce maximum benefit, if an appropriate balance is struck between the pursuit of a searching and penetrating enquiry and the maintenance of an atmosphere of mutual respect and support. Once such a working relationship is created with line management, and others affected by the assignment, it needs to be maintained throughout.

The assignment officer must always keep in mind the overall aim of increasing the efficiency and effectiveness of administration. This objective should be interpreted widely and take into account the purpose of the task examined, its interrelation with departmental objectives and, most importantly, whether it is necessary. Such issues can be large, have wide implications, and may be beyond the direct concern or responsibility of an individual manager, even at senior levels. In such circumstances persistent and penetrative investigation is required, that will demand high personal qualities of the assignment officer. To ensure assignment recommendations are indeed going to increase efficiency and effectiveness, it is essential that they are assessed in cost benefit terms before commitment to implement them is made. This should be done even if it is not possible fully to state all the costs and benefits quantatively. It is also true that, because the assignment officer is concerned with effectiveness as well as efficiency, it may be necessary to recommend additional costs, or to balance gains from cost reduction against the need to provide an effective service. It would be wrong to think the only consideration is to reduce costs. The balance struck between cost containment, and the provision of an effective or improved service, is of course, a matter of judgement to be made in individual situations by the assignment officer and management.

The specialist's approach must be systematic and impartial. The questions what?, why?, when?, where?, and who? must be posed with an open mind. The possibility of an outcome that involves considerable change, in work, personnel, or even the discontinuation of function, should never be ruled out because of the problems or personalities involved.

The provision of realistic advice that is capable of implementation is also of paramount importance. If assignments are not directed towards this end they have no purpose and are an unnecessary cost. The acceptance of recommendations made by assignment officers depends on:

- the intrinsic worth of the advice;
- the skill of the specialist in formulating the advice and getting it accepted; and
- the importance and priority which management attaches to dealing with the issues involved.

A vital aspect of the task of achieving acceptability lies in the identification of the key parties involved and in effective consultation with them. Advice must be acceptable to senior management in principle, but also to operational management in that it is capable of implementation. The views of the trade unions involved may also have to be taken into account. But these considerations do not outweigh the need for objectivity, and the real skill of the specialist lies in gaining acceptance of appropriate recommendations.

Such complexity demonstrates clearly the need for regular review and discussion meetings with clients during the course of an investigation, to ensure that continued agreement on how to proceed exists between those involved. It also points to the importance of defining and agreeing clear terms of reference at the beginning of an assignment. This approach can only be applied circumspectly when a project is imposed by management. Where a potential project is not imposed, and there are fundamental differences of approach among involved parties, careful appraisal of its ultimate viability is necessary before it is agreed to proceed beyond a preliminary study.

Effective implementation is a prime and important objective. One of the best means of achieving it is, of course, to provide sound and acceptable advice; but there is more to it than this, for much can go wrong as a result of a poorly planned implementation programme. An assignment must be well structured and its proposals should include an action document to which the organisation is committed. During the implementation phase contact with the client should be maintained over a wide range of issues, particularly in regard to the provision of training and the resolution of immediate day-to-day problems. A suitable mechanism for monitoring the implementation of recommendations over an agreed timescale must be set up.

4 Types of assignment

Assignments can vary widely in form and content, which range from studies of small office procedures to the large scale application of information technology, or the overall review of organisation. The work involved may necessitate the formation of a multi-disciplinary team, or collaboration with external consultants. Increased management accountability will help to stimulate demand for reviews concerned with overall efficiency and effectiveness as well as investigations of specific operations. Some assignments give rise to far-reaching changes while others produce a number of small, but nevertheless worthwhile, improvements as the result of painstaking and thorough examination of detail by the assignment officer.

5 Assignment management

The basic elements of planning and managing assignments are universally applicable whatever their context. It is of course for senior management services managers in collaboration with top management to decide the overall use and deployment of assignment resources. The former have to judge the cost effectiveness of potential projects, agree terms of reference with senior clients, and determine the level and extent of resources required as well as the timescale of operation.

A project or assignment manager then has to be appointed to oversee the work. This responsibility involves providing management and guidance to assignment staff, and accountability for the preparation, maintenance, and effectiveness of a completion plan drawn up in conformity with the principles outlined in chapter II. This plan is the framework around which the manager's job revolves and, once established, the assignment officer should proceed with detailed investigation. The manager should of course control the allocation and use of resources, monitor progress, and be directly involved at several key points. These are where:

- the framework is set up and the terms of reference of any preliminary study agreed;

- any preliminary survey is complete and action on it is to be decided;
- terms of reference and the timetable are finally agreed with clients;
- assignment staff need help, or outside assistance from other disciplines may be necessary;
- proposals are formulated and first put to clients;
- reports are formally presented to clients; and
- important stages of implementation and follow-up are reached.

The manager may need to participate in early fieldwork and subsequent interviews in order to gain insights into key issues and needs. The manager must also ensure the assignment officer costs each discrete element of the activities examined, establishes the value they add by way of efficiency or effectiveness, and prepares a statement of the savings and benefits expected from the recommendations for inclusion in report findings. Where these are unquantifiable they should be stated as precisely as possible. Sometimes individual elements can only be justified in the context of the whole task, and the calculation of costs, expected benefits and savings, should take account of this fact, when necessary. For example, a particular recommendation may only be practicable if a much wider range of recommendations is implemented, or, alternatively, some individual improvements can be made.

Table 1 outlines how general changes intended to raise the levels of management accountability may affect the operation of management services. As the direct accountability of line management increases the provision of management services is likely to become more closely integrated with supporting the fulfilment of management operations and objectives. The separate management services disciplines will need to work more closely together because some of the advice required by management needs to be of a general nature for a particular area of operations.

Table 1 **Impact of increased line management accountability for resources on the operation of management services**

Less direct line management accountability for resources	More direct line management accountability for resources
a. Management services unit responsible to the Establishment or Finance Officer who, under top management, is directly responsible for the efficient organisation of a department.	a. The role of central management services management is more concerned to support top management by devising, monitoring and controlling management information systems and budgetary controls, and investigating operating problems.
b. Assignments arise by invitation only, except where cyclic review operates, and are directed by senior management services staff. Assignments are mainly concerned with separate parts of the management process.	b. Monitoring work increases, as a result of improved management information systems. More assignments will be concerned with advising on overall management operations, at either the instruction of top management, or the request of individual line managers.
c. O&M, Staff Inspection, and Internal Audit operate separately, although inter-linkage between O&M and Staff Inspection, and also with Operational Research and other disciplines does occur.	c. O&M, Staff Inspection, and possibly Internal Audit or other disciplines, operate under common management but remain separate disciplines.
d. Each assignment is managed by a project manager working within a specific management services discipline.	d. The use of joint project teams bringing together O&M, Staff Inspection, Internal Audit and other disciplines, increases.

CHAPTER II: THE ASSIGNMENT OVERVIEW: BRINGING ABOUT CHANGE

1 What to plan for, and why

This chapter is devoted to aspects of general importance in making assignment work effective, and helps to put the detailed discussion of chapters III to VIII into perspective. Its principal objective is to encourage a disciplined and planned approach to two key concerns: the relationship of assignments to their wider environmental setting, and secondly, thorough project planning. Careful attention to these matters will almost certainly increase the likelihood of effective implementation, because they promote correct response to, and management of, needs and attitudes.

One snare to be avoided throughout the life of assignments is over-concentration on technical details. This often results in failure to perceive the overall circumstances and wider requirements of the client. It also lowers the likelihood of securing any change involved smoothly, and may lead to useful proposals being rejected. More prominence is being given, both within management services disciplines and line management, to positive planning in assignment work for acceptance of change. There are several reasons for this development. The need to maximise the efficient use of management services resources is one; projects and reports which do not lead to results have clearly occupied resources which could be better used elsewhere, and probably involve lost opportunity. The increased rate of technological development is another. If the potential of technical innovations is to be exploited to the full, assignment staff must be skilled at handling the implementation of changes in working practices and procedures associated with them.

Effective planning of the work is a basic necessity in all assignments and this should include planning for change, which is discussed more fully in the following section. The preparation of a completion plan provides the assignment officer with a most important tool which is outlined in detail in section 3 of this chapter. A plan provides a concrete framework within which to operate, and for pulling together individual stages. It can be a valuable communications aid with the client, especially if it has been constructed jointly. A completion plan encourages problems which arise during an assignment to be dealt with in a planned integrated way. It also enables the requirement for resources to be established reasonably accurately. Perhaps most important of all, it identifies clearly the commitment required to the assignment objectives, both from the client and the assignment officer's own management.

An element in planning that on no account should be overlooked is that concerned with implementation. In the past the importance of this has not been emphasised sufficiently, and assignment staff have tended to see their contribution ending with the issuing of a report and recommendations. It is in fact essential that an adequate plan is made to implement the assignment, and details about this are outlined in Chapter VIII.

2 Bringing about change

It is not uncommon for thought to be given to the implementation of changes that arise out of assignment work only when specific problems emerge, which tends to be at a late stage. If serious difficulties then develop much of the earlier effort may be wasted. This type of loss can be minimised, if not avoided, with forethought and willingness on the part of the assignment officer to approach the assignment in a manner which facilitates the acceptance of change. Two disciplines in particular help in this respect.

The first is conscious planning to achieve change. It is essential to pay as much attention to planning for its achievement as to other aspects of an assignment. Plans for change should form an integral part of overall assignment planning. Assignment staff should have a keen awareness of the importance of their role in helping to achieve change effectively, and how important this is in making assignments successful. Effort needs to be made early in an assignment to identify what change is likely to arise and what plans are necessary to achieve it. It is very important that provision is made to consider planning for change at the entry stage, especially in the context of terms of reference and the preliminary study.

The second discipline which helps secure change is the way in which day-to-day work of the assignment is conducted. The skills required can only be gained by experience and training. Ability to relate to people is very important, for it is a great help in successfully identifying and 'selling' the overall objective contained in the assignment. A participative style is the most appropriate; the assignment officer must be prepared to listen seriously to the thoughts and ideas of others and be willing to evolve the eventual recommendations in discussion with the client. This process involves dialogue and should promote client ownership of suitable proposals. The more complicated the assignment, and the bigger the issues which affect acceptance of change, the greater is the need for an open approach. It is of course not always practicable to proceed in such a way, and the feasibility of doing so should be considered at a very early stage in an assignment. The participative approach is nearly always the one to aim for, and should be adopted unless there are compelling reasons for not doing so. In some assignments it may only be possible to deal with certain aspects in this way. Issues in an assignment which may cause significant change should be taken into account, and given systematic attention, throughout the life of an assignment. Relationships between client, assignment officer, the assignment officer's own management, and those being affected by change, all need to be considered.

Because matters related to the change process tend to be important, and different, at particular progress points, the remaining paragraphs of this section are devoted to the indication of those key points, and the issues that are particularly appropriate to each. The points are identified in relation to the assignment stages or phases used later in the book, and are cross referenced to the paragraphs where their full purpose is outlined.

At entry (Chapter III, section 2)

It is obviously sensible to ensure all relevant issues are considered at this stage. If it is justified a preliminary survey should be made which takes specific account of aspects that might raise acceptance difficulties. Careful attention should always be paid to the questions listed below at this point in an assignment.

- Are the reasons for the assignment wholly those mentioned by the client?
- Are there others that the client only understands partly or is totally unaware of?

- Is there a mechanism for resolving points of conflict between client and assignment officer?
- What will be the final status of the recommendations?

It is most important that potential difficulties in bringing about change are explored so they can be dealt with in a planned way from the start. Special effort should be made to understand the background reasons for their existence. Meetings held with the client and job holders should be used to explore potential acceptance difficulties, identify as precisely as possible what the client wishes to achieve, and constraints being imposed by the client, or being put upon the client by others. Where there are multiple clients it is especially important to identify areas of difference between them. It is essential to extend investigation beyond the immediate client if the assignment's impact is likely to be widespread, to ensure all perspectives are understood and evaluated. This may involve taking account of departmental and Service-wide considerations. At the entry stage the primary objective should be to find out the degree of identity between local aims and the requirements of senior management or customers, identify the overall level of desire for change, explore organisational implications, and gain knowledge of the ability of all the parties involved to work together. A strategy for dealing with change issues should be defined which should have a major influence on the preparation of the completion plan.

When the contract is drawn up (Chapter III, section 3)

Objectives and completion plans should be jointly developed unless the circumstances of the study make this impossible. Working participatively aids agreement and helps to minimise misunderstandings. The involvement of senior or top management, as appropriate, should also be gained in this process, particularly to ensure they understand their own role and to confirm their agreement to the proposed approach to assignment completion. Failure to achieve this can lead to confusion, misunderstanding, and waste of time among those involved. Where several parties are concerned with an assignment, it is necessary to define individual roles and responsibilities and ensure that they are properly understood. This also helps to promote a sense of common purpose and avoids confusion. If the assignment is relatively straightforward these matters can be dealt with informally, otherwise they should be settled systematically through agreed channels. It may not be possible to maintain undertakings reached at the preliminary stage throughout the life of an assignment. If subsequent events point to the need for revision of the contract this should of course be done, provided the alteration is agreed with all those involved. If agreement is not possible termination of the assignment must be considered, and the shortcomings likely to result if necessary revisions to the contract are not made should be registered clearly with the client.

During diagnosis and analysis (Chapter IV)

It is during this stage that relationships are developed with staff directly involved with, and affected by, the assignment. This can happen at formal interviews or in informal discussion. From the latter in particular can come invaluable information about operational troubles or individual working difficulties. Considerable benefit can result from adopting a consultative approach, in which the assignment officer tests and evolves personal ideas and incorporates these with those of others. Sensible ideas and views derived from practical experience should be responded to, whatever their source. The encouragement of communication and discussion can in itself be a great help in the process of gaining acceptance of change. People who feel involved and have had their own ideas taken into account or accepted are much more likely to respond favourably to proposals which affect their way of working.

In seeking agreement (Chapter VI, section 3)

This is a critical stage in the completion of an assignment. It is important at this point to ensure proposals do not emerge at a formal presentation, or in a written report, without being discussed previously. There is advantage in developing solutions and proposals openly; this promotes acceptance of change and ensures that final proposals contain a minimum of items unfamiliar to the client. Contentious and difficult proposals should not be left to emerge at a late stage unless this is thought to be a sensible tactic; in fact their very difficulty usually makes it all the more important to bring them into the open as early as possible. Early consideration during this stage, about how implementation will be planned, will help to allay any fears the client has, and create confidence in the proposals.

During implementation (Chapter VIII)

If it is made clear to the client that support will be given while implementation proceeds, the client's confidence to manage the change process will usually be boosted. The following measures are particularly helpful in this respect: make a gradual planned withdrawal so that support in the application of new and unfamiliar practices is not lost suddenly; assist with the training and education of staff in introducing new arrangements; continue to advise on implementation problems as long as this is reasonable.

Table 2 **Points to promote when the completion plan is drawn up**

a. Ensure requirements are defined clearly and precisely.

b. Only accept reasonable deadlines.

c. Ensure communications are adequate. Ensure individuals are identified who will communicate with the staff and with the staff side.

d. Ensure provision is made for the escalation of costs.

e. Ensure resources, of cash or people, are sufficient to complete the assignment.

f. Ensure assignment staff are experienced and appropriately deployed.

g. Ensure internal political problems are faced and resolved.

h. Ensure provision is made to appraise progress at key points and take 'stop' or 'go' decisions.

3 The completion plan: achieving overall control

A completion plan which gives attention to the factors outlined in Table 2 will help to avoid many of the pitfalls that can arise during an assignment. The following principles should govern the preparation and operation of the completion plan. First, an initial appraisal of the assignment should be made to break it into appropriate component parts and identify the main issues to be resolved. This discipline will also help to estimate the resources needed. Secondly, the assignment should have a specific and clear plan drawn up for its completion. Thirdly, it should be ensured that assignment work proceeds methodically in relation to the stages and completion plan previously defined. The basic divisions of most types of assignment are reflected in the headings of sections II to V of this book; namely, Getting Started, Analysis and Diagnosis, Planning for Action, and Implementation. The typical pattern of assignment work is illustrated in Figure 1.

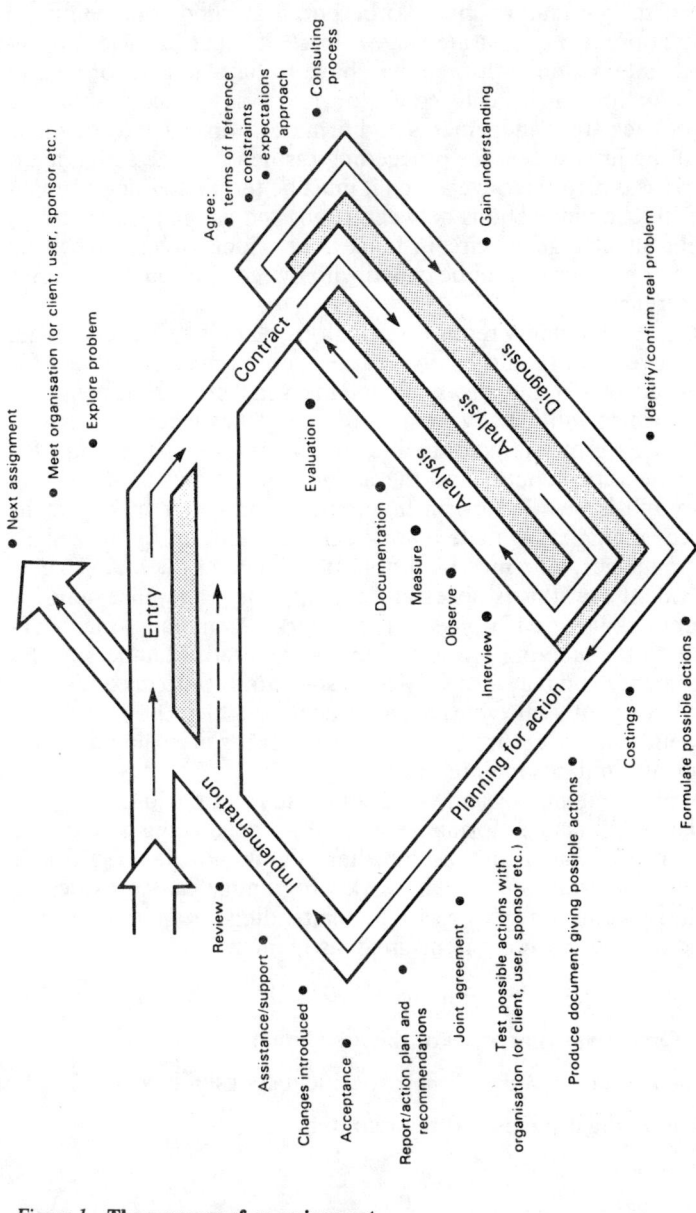

Figure 1 **The sequence of an assignment**

Two special features need to be borne in mind concerning the completion of the separate stages. First, if other agencies are involved interaction with them will have to be planned, for lack of co-ordination can lead to confusion and delay. Secondly, at the end of each stage judgements and firm decisions have to be made about the justification for proceeding further with the assignment. If serious difficulties have arisen it must be terminated, eg a breakdown in communications between client and assignment officer, a significant change in circumstances, or wider issues have been opened up which cannot be coped with by redefinition of the terms of reference.

Large assignments require scrupulous planning at every stage. Policy oversight should be divided formally from responsibility for day-to-day work, and may be vested in a small group, the composition of which will, ideally, remain the same throughout the assignment. This group is accountable for the resources used and for major decisions concerning the assignment. It acts as a steering group and is best led by an independent or senior management services manager. Detailed work can be overseen by an assignment manager, who may be different for each of the main stages. The extent that this is necessary depends on the requirement for different skills at each phase of the work. Assignment managers report to the steering group if one is appointed. Members of the assignment team may also vary from stage to stage to maximise the use of relevant skills. Large assignments ought to be monitored independently to ensure that the client's needs are being met and technical standards maintained.

Smaller assignments and work completed by individuals have to be planned much less formally, the precise need being a matter of judgement in each situation, but there should always be sufficient planning to establish a clear work programme and provide for monitoring and control. Precise understanding is required, in writing, about the following items in all assignments.

- Agreed terms of reference.
- Objectives (purpose) of the assignment.
- Parties involved and their specific responsibilities.
- Individual stages and their content.
- Timescales.
- Specific review points.

- Role of top management and their formal agreement to the completion plan.
- Resources required.

The acquisition and deployment of necessary skills should be positively planned, either by the creation of a representative team, or through individual initiatives by the assignment officer.

CHAPTER III: GETTING STARTED

1 Basic issues to be resolved

Getting going is never easy. Right at the start of an assignment there may be little or no information, or contacts available, about the work to be completed – the proverbial 'blank sheet of paper'. Circumstances however are not often that difficult, and usually at least the basic contacts are known and some information is available. What is almost certain to be absent is any structure to the assignment, and the main objective at this stage is to identify one and establish it formally in a suitable contract before any work is started. Consideration should also be given to the proposed assignment's viability.

Unless time and energy is given to the creation of a framework within which to proceed, it is difficult to make any progress at all. The effort should also be more than a token amount. The start point is the one stage when all parties are prepared to think about the objectives and tactical planning required to achieve them. Bear in mind it may be difficult to correct shortcomings later, both because people will be concerned with other matters by then, and because initial views, once agreed, tend to become difficult to change. If priorities, requirements, or plans are not established clearly at the beginning, unnecessary complications are more likely to occur while the assignment is in progress.

2 Entry

Entry work includes all the activities associated with the preliminary evaluation of an assignment. It can be categorised under three heads, which may be carried out simultaneously or sequentially, depending on the circumstances. If there is uncertainty about the viability of a proposed assignment, or about what is required to be done, the preliminary survey will clearly take a higher priority than if the assignment is straightforward and obviously necessary.

Background work. It is important to gain a good understanding as quickly as possible about the background to the proposed assignment, and this can be obtained from information already documented and direct discussion with the client. Information on the client's understanding of objectives, activities and procedures should be gathered, together with as much quantitative and financial detail as is readily available on current and past performance. At this stage it is essential that fundamental issues are considered and such questions as, 'is this organisation still fulfilling its purpose?', and, 'is the organisation's stated purpose valid?', or, 'even if the overall purpose is appropriate is it being met effectively and efficiently?', should be raised. Questions of this type have direct relevance to the agreement of terms of reference, which in the final form need to be realistic and deal effectively with the real issues to be tackled.

Initial contacts. How these are made is crucial to the success of an assignment. It is certainly a difficult time if the work is being done without the willing acceptance of local line management. But it is not necessarily easier just because the client has invited the investigation. The initial reception is likely to be friendly, but if the client's view about issues turns out to be different to the perspectives developed by the assignment staff, this atmosphere may not last. Acceptable proposals will then only be produced by persistent and tactful efforts to understand and influence the client's position. It is very important that understanding and mutual respect between assignment staff and client are achieved, which will help to lay the foundations of amicable relationships throughout its course. At this point assignment staff need to familiarise themselves with the client's concerns and problems, and the client has to ensure those needs are communicated effectively to them. This can be a delicate process, particularly where the issues are complex, subtle or not clearly understood.

A proportion of the initial liaison will be handled or led by senior management services staff, but at some point the assignment officer will need to take an increasingly active part, preferably at an early stage.

Preliminary survey. This can be a valuable mechanism to aid understanding, and generally make provision for the overall structure of the assignment. It is always wise to undertake a preliminary survey where the issues which surround an assignment are complex, incompletely understood, or subject to dispute, although it may not be necessary where the justification for the assignment is clearly understood or is part of regular audit work.

The main purpose of a preliminary survey is to clarify understanding about the problems. It can also help to decide how to conduct the detailed investigation, as a clear understanding can be obtained of what information is required to complete the assignment. A preliminary survey can additionally be used to assess the assignment's potential value. If rough costings of activities, overall and by relevant sub-categories, are collected it is possible to estimate the likely savings and gains that will arise. If the gains are modest and assignment staff could be used more profitably elsewhere, no further work should be completed.

A preliminary survey can also be used by assignment staff to check the client's understanding of problems and possible solutions, particularly to establish if there are any hidden issues which require attention. The importance of these should not be under-estimated, for there are occasions when matters of this type require urgent attention, and are of greater significance than those which led to the investigation in the first place. Sometimes the resolution of hidden issues materially affects the approach required to deal with the openly identified problems. Difficulties encountered in gaining acceptance of new working practices can prove to be intractable, and are not necessarily obvious from discussion with the client.

A preliminary survey need only take a day or two to complete, although it could take longer if the issues are complex.

Work done at the entry phase leads towards, and culminates in, the preparation of a completion plan for the conduct of the assignment. The plan should be based on knowledge currently available of issues, problems, and proposals likely to emerge. It should identify the resources required to complete the assignment. Use should be made of the planning process discussed in the previous section. Unless there are very pressing reasons to prevent it the plan needs to be mutually agreeable to assignment staff and client, and its substance influenced by the requirements and situation which exist locally. A completion plan of some kind ought always to be agreed, together with at least one review point at which assignment viability should be considered. Progress beyond the conclusion of the contract stage, to the commencement of detailed work, should not occur unless a plan of the kind previously outlined is prepared and agreed.

3 Contract

Once satisfactory agreement is reached about the viability and purpose of an assignment this should be set out in writing and not left as an imprecise, and possibly confused, understanding of objectives and how they will be achieved. This action amounts to the preparation of a contract which is, in fact, the formal conclusion of 'getting started'.

The contract has several distinct components which may be kept separate or built into a comprehensive agreement, whichever is the most appropriate. However brief or informal the contract is it should always be committed to writing. The individual components to be included and clarified are outlined below.

Background. There should be a statement which outlines why the assignment is needed.

The terms of reference. These state the objective of the assignment, as agreed between assignment staff and the client. They require careful consideration and take into account the outcome of the preliminary survey, if made, and background work. The terms of reference should state what the parties concerned see as reasonable and realistic objectives for the assignment, and should take account of any relevant union agreements.

What will be examined, and how. This establishes clearly the work areas to be examined, the practices, structures and procedures involved, and the methods to be used.

The resources required and time allowed. These matters are of concern to the assignment staff in order to ensure adequate resources are available, especially if an end or target date is to be established. The client is interested because they are the most visible and concrete signs of commitment to the assignment on the part of those who are to conduct it. A clear statement of the need for, and availability of resources, and time required, helps to put a precise framework around an assignment.

Action to be taken by interested parties. The client and the assignment officer must of course be clear about each other's role and their interrelationship. Costly confusion can arise between them over the management of resources, the assignment team's responsibility, and how the proposals should be implemented. There are also a number of other interested parties who can be involved in an assignment. These include senior management, in both management services and line management, who, although they often do not participate directly in an assignment, are interested and influential in its progress. This is especially true in the following contexts: the agreement of objectives, the provision of positive support, and the implementation of recommendations which emerge. Their role is important, and a contract should not be established without ensuring they agree the terms and objectives proposed. There are several reasons why this rule should be observed. If senior line management is not clearly supportive of an assignment waste of time and resources can easily result. This will happen if assignment staff repeatedly have to establish entry to different levels or groups of management within a single organisation, because senior management has not given clear instruction about the existence of the assignment, or the support to be given to assignment staff. The situation to be avoided at all costs, is that in which recommendations are unacceptable to senior line management because their interests and objectives have not been identified clearly enough. Trade unions may also be involved, and if this is so their views and comments need to be taken account of throughout the assignment in an informal way, and formally at key stages.

Provisions for planning and monitoring. In one form or another, an agreement should be reached as to how the provisions outlined in the previous section for conducting and monitoring assignments are to be applied. If the project is a simple one the understanding reached can be relatively straightforward and informal, but the minimum provision outlined on page 26 of this book should always be applied.

CHAPTER IV: ANALYSIS AND DIAGNOSIS

1 The need for a logical approach

This chapter addresses two fundamental issues associated with the collection and analysis of information. Initially it outlines guidance on the collection and usage of data, and secondly, it sets out the steps to be followed in a sound analytical method. In chapter V some techniques that are useful in analysis and diagnosis are outlined, together with an indication of the contribution which each can make.

It is worth paying careful attention to the way in which investigatory work is completed. A logical approach should be adopted because it promotes thorough and organised appraisal of the issues and problems, and enables the real needs and objectives of the assignment to be identified. If the work of the assignment officer is disorganised, it is likely that insufficient information will be collected and the issues will be incompletely understood. This may, in turn, lead to the adoption of superficial solutions. The method advocated in this chapter has two main characteristics, which are briefly, to proceed from the general to the particular, and from the top downwards. The generic term 'macro' covers issues which need to be assessed primarily in global terms, and 'micro' relates to detailed considerations.* There are clearly other ways of defining an analytical method, and no particular model framework can always be applied to the letter. Real life situations are often not capable of tidy definition in any case. In practice it is necessary to identify the best starting point and most practicable approach. But the particular method outlined serves two important purposes.

---

* These terms can be applied in any context whether it be a branch or a whole government department.

First, it helps to emphasise in principle the importance of logical analysis. Secondly, attention is drawn to the tendency in assignment work to lose sight of wider issues and over-emphasise 'nuts and bolts' matters.

The objective of analysis is to identify and understand accurately the detail of organisational structures, how people are deployed, procedures, and their associated strengths and weaknesses. This is most likely to be achieved successfully if analysis proceeds from the general to the particular. At the same time the likelihood of following blind alleys, and becoming bogged down in a mass of apparently unconnected detail is reduced significantly. This method of analysis also allows for evaluation of the length and value of the assignment to be made, as well as the environmental context in which it is set.

The framework outlined above is of course an ideal one and reality does not always allow it to be followed absolutely. An assignment may only be concerned with detailed issues, the more general ones having already been resolved, or known not to require investigation. Sometimes it is only possible to begin an assignment in a particular detailed area, or it is politic to begin in this way, in anticipation that the work will lead to a wider study. On other occasions it is necessary to complete certain detailed work in order to clarify requirements at a more general level. Practical pressures sometimes divert attention from the ideal, a fact which serves to heighten the value of the model framework, for it is in such circumstances that the potential dangers in not following a structured approach can easily materialise. All these considerations demonstrate the importance of judgement in deciding the best way forward, and a sound framework to work within furthers the likelihood that good judgements are made. The value of a model framework lies in the power it has to maintain a sense of order and perspective in completing an analysis. It is still relevant even if an assignment is known to be mainly concerned with detailed matters. If detail is considered without any regard to wider issues, proposals may be unrealistic.

Logical analysis is of inestimable value in assignment work but it sometimes fails to provide solutions to problems. When this occurs it can be very useful to experiment with various techniques designed to help produce ideas. Collectively such techniques are known as creative thinking, brainstorming being a particularly well-known one. More is written about creative thinking in chapter V.

2 Data collection and evaluation

No analytical process can be successful unless founded on soundly collected and evaluated data. It is therefore important to give attention to both matters.

The prime purpose of gathering data is to make objective checks and tests on current work practices, or proposed changes. Ultimately, the data collected is used to justify the proposals which emerge from an assignment. So all the knowledge required to prepare sound proposals needs to be obtained, although effort should be made to avoid the accumulation of unnecessary data. Account should also be taken of practical limitations on time or other constraints.

Careful thought should be given at the beginning of an assignment to what data is required, and how detailed it will have to be. It is wise initially to identify the most detailed level and anticipate collection at that level. There are very good reasons why this stance should be adopted. It ensures nothing is missed and that once data is collected it will not be necessary to resift records, or other sources, at later stages in the work. It is often difficult to gain access to sources twice in an assignment. However, the principle of collecting at the most detailed level should not be followed blindly, and if it becomes clear as work proceeds that this is unnecessary, an appropriate adjustment should be made. Constraints on time and resources can limit the overall usefulness or reliability of the data it will be possible to collect. If real difficulties develop about ability to secure data at the level of detail required consideration should be given to discontinuing the assignment. At the same time as identifying what data is essential, thought should be given to how and from whom it can be obtained.

There are several key principles to take into account when data is collected.

- Be systematic.
- Only use data gathered by yourself or confirmed by authoritative sources.
- Separate facts from opinions.
- Obtain typical data, by the use of sampling if possible.

The most difficult of these principles to fulfil is the third one. To stress the need to separate fact and opinion does not imply the value of opinions is decried. They can be very valuable, for they provide ideas for solving the issues under investigation and clues to the source of problems. But opinions are often communicated as though they are facts, and if the material is to be fully utilised the assignment officer must be able to separate the one from the other, since fact and opinion are quite different types of information and are used in different ways.

When data is collected there are a number of key questions to be asked about tasks performed, and the level of accuracy obtained from replies to each should be evaluated and noted.

What is done? The aim of the question is to identify the process and its end-product.

Can it be measured? Always challenge, albeit discreetly, views which suggest that measurement is impossible.

Why is it done? Always remember the function or activity may be partly or wholly inessential.

Who does it? This question opens up discussion about the allocation of people to tasks and their suitability.

When is it done? Most activity either contains or is part of a cycle or larger process, and it may be possible to order component parts with greater efficiency.

Where is it done? There may be scope for the rationalisation of the location where the work is done.

How is it done? There is need to examine the methods adopted, the staff and work movements involved, equipment used and the management structure, etc.

Who else is affected? This will help to ensure that background issues, perhaps not readily apparent, are taken into account.

There are many ways by which data can be obtained and none that are potentially useful should be neglected. Several are commonly applied and therefore worth specific mention.

- Formal documents, either as published or working papers are clearly a major source of data. In published papers any facts given are preselected and can be difficult to check, but they provide useful background, especially if successive related documents are available over a period of time. Formally agreed procedures, as well as organisation charts are generally available. Actual working papers are more valuable than formally produced documents, because they offer

the opportunity to examine unselected material. Analysis of such documents can help to clarify the nature of the problems which exist, and how they might be resolved. Data about work completed, workflow, and work procedures, including time taken up by different activities, can also be obtained.
- It is also possible to observe directly the activity under examination and the people who perform it. Useful insights can be obtained and unclear details about the work can be checked.
- Perhaps the principal sources of knowledge are interviews and discussion. Understanding about purposes, relationships, staff morale, and indeed factual detail, can often only be obtained through direct questions. It is also very frequently the only way to find out exactly what is done, and how it is divided up between all those involved. Interviewing additionally is a prime method for obtaining the involvement of job holders in the development of solutions, although this may happen through informal discussion opened up by the interview, rather than at the interview itself.
- Sampling can be beneficial when there is need to identify the principal characteristics and divisions within a large mass of detail. It can either provide enough data on which to base recommendations, or indicate the direction and amount of further fact finding necessary.
- Questionnaires can also be used, particularly where a large number of individuals need to be canvassed about a single issue, or on a number of detailed points. To be of real value much thought needs to be given to the construction of the questionnaire. Issues which relate to how questions are phrased, the use of alternative answer questions, the use of degrees of agreement, and provision for free comment by respondents, all have to be considered. Clarity of structure is especially important if it is not possible to ask personal supplementary questions. The questionnaire is most reliable where only basic and factual data is required. Questionnaires are not very effective where complex issues must be assessed, and if used in such contexts, usually have to be augmented by individual interviews.

Once acquired, data has to be collected and summarised if it is to be used effectively, and there are a number of techniques which assist in this process. One of the most important is note taking which occurs at or after interviews. Everyone has a different style and approach, but there are one or two general points of advice that are important to remember when this technique is used. Always make some record of the date, place, and the names of those present at meetings or interviews. The value of a series of notes can be greatly reduced if they cannot be put into sequential order after a lapse in time, and it can be useful to know who has been present on a particular occasion. Always make a record of an important discussion or development as soon after it has happened as possible.

Charting is a valuable method of displaying large amounts of detailed data in a way which is informative, and helpful for analysis purposes. This method is particularly desirable when there is a need to plot the flow of events or procedures.

The preparation of organisation charts, which include a breakdown to individual jobs and their specification, can be a very useful means of recording how work is done and distributed. This practice also helps to determine whether any rationalisation of job content is necessary.

Data can also be put in order by means of statistical analysis. It is useful to know, for instance, if data is subject to cyclical variations, since that will affect proposals concerned with the control of the tasks involved. Data can be summarised in statistical tables or graphs and charts, all of which help the analysis of the data. Tests for statistical significance can be helpful in determining the value of data. Such aids bring clarity to the interpretation of data if used correctly.

Another source of help, in both the storage and analysis of data, are proprietary computer programs developed for specific purposes. Availability of such programs together with microcomputers, means that basic analyses and calculations can be made much more quickly, easily, and comprehensively than was possible in the past.

References in this section to ways in which data is collected, and techniques that are useful in analysing it, are very brief and are only intended as a basic introduction. More details about some of them are to be found in chapter V, although reference to specialised books is necessary to gain deeper understanding.

3 Analysis

An important stage in any analysis is background investigation.

This can be most enlightening where the assignment is the latest in a series of studies. The examination of earlier reports can help to eradicate certain lines of enquiry which have been found to be unproductive in the past, although the conclusions reached on previous occasions should not be responded to without further enquiry. Other background information should also be obtained, if available. Work at this point may involve some direct contact with the client to gather written material, and also the client's own perspective about the background to the assignment. Meetings with the client can also be used to check understandings gained from other sources, and the assignment officer's own ideas. This sort of investigation ought to be made primarily at the beginning of an assignment to appraise wider needs, but can be repeated with profit during analysis. It will help to identify the main issues, and the lines of enquiry that will be necessary when detailed work begins.

The model framework advocated to assist detailed analysis is a two-staged process which begins at the macro-level, and moves progressively to look at more detailed issues, although this is obviously subject to the modifications discussed in section 1 of this chapter. It is expressed in organisational terms because most management services analysis occurs within this broad context. There are very good reasons for planning the analysis in this way. The objective of any analysis is to help achieve a rational and effective solution, and this is most likely to be secured when a structured framework is used.

To move from the general to the particular makes it more likely that all possible solutions will be examined, and that the various strands of the enquiry will be kept in perspective. If the problem is tackled in an unstructured way, or the investigation is built up from the bottom without due regard being given to the overall picture, the likelihood of an incomplete or distorted outcome is considerably increased. The possibility of getting lost in detail, and perhaps even following a blind alley becomes considerably greater. Initially, questions at both macro and micro level will tend to be directed towards the assembly of facts on key issues, but as the assignment progresses there will be more and more desire to seek answers and test ideas.

The analysis of macro issues is fundamentally concerned with the investigation of the overall management strategy, and its relationship with the structures, procedures and staff usage being examined. The basic questions to be raised are, 'is the required objective being met?', and, 'if so, is the overall strategy identified to achieve it the most appropriate?'. Ideas which the assignment officer has developed need to be tested in discussion with management, job holders and customers, because they all have important insights into the tasks at hand. There are three dimensions to be considered when questions are asked.

Organisation. The key issue, is 'are the major divisions within the structure, and the breakdown of responsibilities within these, the most effective to meet the strategy laid down by management?'. If the structure is inappropriate and there is mismatch between it and the needs of the organisation, confusion will result. This is likely to cause problems in communication, conflict between individual post holders, delay, poor morale and general ineffectiveness.

Procedures. The key issue is, 'are these defined in a way which maximises support of the overall strategy?'. Procedures are an essential part of any work process. They provide the detailed framework within which the work is done. It is very important that they complement organisation structure efficiently. If they do not the same sorts of difficulties arise as when the organisation structure is ineffective. Incorrect procedures can have an adverse effect on the organisation's operation. Confusion and mis-management can result if top management is not receiving the information required to control the organisation, or does not receive it at the appropriate times.

People. The key issue is, with emphasis on those filling management positions, 'are the right people available with the right skills?'. People are a major consideration in the execution of most tasks and yet their role is often taken for granted. When the part played by individuals is assessed the issue of dealing with 'misfits' is not the paramount interest, although of course this can be a real problem and require resolution. The essential concern is with the identification of the need for people with particular qualities and skills. If shortages or imbalances are identified, an indication of what training is required to make people more able to fulfil the role required of them must be provided.

Micro-analysis is basically concerned with how the overall strategy is applied in detail. It is therefore of considerable value to have some clear ideas about overall purpose, structure, and design of procedures before this phase is embarked upon. If an assignment is concerned with macro questions and no satisfactory understanding is being reached about them, the worth of proceeding any further should be questioned, although in the end it may be beneficial to do so. It is possible that detailed work will help to clarify the broader issues, and if this turns out to be the case, there is every reason why the assignment should be successful.

Micro-analysis also has three dimensions, and to a large extent the principles addressed are the same as at the macro level, although the emphasis is on detail.

Organisation. The key issue is, 'are individual jobs and responsibilities structured and graded appropriately, and are there an appropriate number of management levels in the hierarchy?'.

Procedures. The key issue is, 'are operating procedures clear and compatible with the required pattern of jobs and individual duties?'.

People. The key issue is, 'are people available in the right numbers and with the right skills?'.

4 Diagnosis

Good diagnosis comprises an accurate identification of the issues and problems to be resolved. Although this book makes a formal separation between diagnosis and the formulation of proposals there is in fact very close association between the two, and in practice they are frequently not kept consciously separate. Even so it is important to realise that a diagnostic stage does occur, and that if it is faulty the proposals put forward may be superficial or incorrect. A basic weakness in assignment work is the tendency to jump too quickly from analysis to the identification of solutions, without really isolating the problem. What therefore is involved in diagnosis? It consists of an informal weighing and sifting of evidence in order to come to a conclusion. In contrast the formulation of proposals entails putting the conclusions that emerge from diagnosis into a structured detailed form. Diagnosis involves weighing up the various strands of evidence and information that are made available from analysis of the basic data. Some of the strands may be in the form of understandings or impressions rather than hard facts, and diagnosis clearly involves the assignment officer in bringing to bear all his or her training and experience.

Reference to colleagues or the client for guidance may well prove helpful in drawing a final conclusion.

This weighing and sifting process can be assisted by the adoption of a structured approach which involves five tests of the material on which the diagnosis is to be based. The assignment officer should:

- identify what is politically acceptable or unacceptable;
- lay out and weigh the alternative solutions which appear possible;
- assess the scope for increased computerisation;
- make sure that accompanying changes in working practices and potential difficulties in gaining acceptance of each option are identified, at both macro and micro levels; and,
- cost the alternatives, in order to identify the most cost-effective among them.

Cost analysis is an essential element in the diagnosis stage of an assignment but it is not necessarily the only significant factor, for cost considerations may be overriden by policy requirements or other needs. Cost assessments should include an evaluation of benefits even though these may be difficult to quantify.

Once a diagnosis has been made a key stage in any assignment is complete. A major point of decision is involved and from then on it becomes increasingly difficult and costly to change direction. If the diagnosis results in the emergence of several options of approximately equal weight a decision will have to be made about how to proceed. It may be sensible, and practicable, to keep all or a number of the options open as long as possible. But if that is not feasible one of them will have to be selected as that to be adopted, which may well involve considerable discussion about how to proceed, with the client and the assignment officer's own management. Even if the selection of the preferred option is delayed a positive choice will have to be made eventually. The assignment may well have to be discontinued if the diagnosis is not compatible with wider policy or administrative constraints.

CHAPTER V: USEFUL TECHNIQUES

1 Interviewing: basic understanding required

Interviewing is one of the fundamental working tools available to assignment officers, and very few assignments are completed without use being made of it at some stage. Of all the techniques associated with management services work it is the one in which a high degree of skill is most necessary. The degree of attention that needs to be paid to obtaining competence can be underestimated. Since to use this skill requires no special learning, we tend to believe no particular knowledge is required in order to be a good interviewer. This is far from the truth, and even the most expert of interviewers can benefit from a considered appraisal of their technique. The detailed approach to the conduct of an interview needs to be varied according to the purposes of, and circumstances in which, the interview takes place. The need in management services assignments is, for example, different to that which exists when interviewing a welfare claimant from a list of set questions. If interviewing experience has been gained in other contexts it is important, when joining a management services team for the first time, to consider whether an adjustment in style is necessary.

In management services work the interview has three interlinked, but distinct, functions. The three functions are:

- to obtain precise information required to complete the assignment;
- to build up background intelligence which will help in understanding the overall situation under investigation;
- to develop good relationships with the people met in the course of the assignment, in order to promote understanding and co-operation in completing it.

Subtle refinements of approach will be made within this

framework depending on the purpose of the interview. For example, the stance taken at an initial interview with the manager responsible for the area under survey will be different to that adopted at an interview with a subordinate about the work being performed, but all three elements identified above will always be present to some degree.

It is important for the management services interviewer to appreciate that he or she is asking something of the interviewee, and is not usually in a position to demand a response. It is after all the interviewer who has requested the interview and wants something from it. An aggressive or overbearing manner can therefore do nothing to contribute to success, and should always be avoided. Even so the interviewer should not appear over-deferential, and should certainly not be tentative or apologetic. The manner of the interviewer should be professional, but not clinical; friendly, but not over-familiar. Above all the interviewer should appear confident and competent, and be sensitive but neutral in developing a relationship with the interviewee. If the interviewer's overall approach is as suggested above the productiveness of the interview will be maximised, because every encouragement will be given to the interviewee to talk freely. It is when this happens that it is possible to get most out of an interview.

The interviewer has to be clear about the objective to be achieved during the course of the interview, eg what detailed information and understandings are sought from it? If this is muddled the outcome is likely to be unsatisfactory; the interviewer will probably not get the information desired and the interviewee will tend to feel the interview has achieved little, or even been a waste of time. If the interviewee does begin to think in this way the risk that unhelpfulness or obstructiveness might develop is considerably increased.

Finally, successful interviewing depends as much on the ability to listen as the flair to ask questions skilfully. Questions cannot be effective if no account is taken of the answers. Listening is important at several levels; empathy and insight into what lies behind statements is as important as factual comprehension. It is also important to respond to non-verbal messages about feelings, attitudes, fears and hopes, as well as to what is actually said. Listening is not easy and can be inhibited by various factors, which may affect the interviewer as much as the person who is interviewed. Common inhibitors are physical barriers, like noise or interruptions, or distance, but prejudice, assumptions, anxiety, and different understandings of what words mean, can also prevent good listening.

2 The professional interview

When conducting an interview, always have a clear perception of what is to be achieved. Be as informed as possible before the interview starts, and sift relevant background information. This can be obtained from the notes of other interviews, from questionnaires filled in by the interviewee and any other means available. A clear objective is an essential pre-requisite to the conduct of a professional interview.

To know what is aimed at only in general terms is insufficient. A plan must be developed for the achievement of the desired outcome, at the same time as the objective is identified, and probably from the same material. The plan should be flexible. In an interview it is important that the interviewee is allowed to talk freely, and too rigid an interview plan may curtail or prevent this. The best practice is to identify areas of questioning and items of key importance in each, rather than specific questions, and ensure while the interview proceeds that all the areas and items are covered. Individual questions can be framed as necessary. Such an approach provides maximum opportunity for the interviewer to maintain control and get the information required, and also allows the interviewee freedom to comment and respond in an individual way.

The interviewee should always be put at ease if at all possible. The interview situation can create tension and stress, mainly because of the uncertainty involved. It is the responsibility of the interviewer to prevent this, and some practical suggestions to help achieve this are made here. Reliance on jokes to help people relax is not advisable. Not everyone's sense of humour is the same! It is often helpful, however, to have a few minutes' general conversation at the start of an interview. On the assumption that both those involved have not met before, the following practice will do a great deal to ensure it commences, and continues, free of tension. The interviewer should:

- explain the purpose of the interview;
- focus the discussion on the main points;
- conduct the interview in a straightforward and business-like manner;
- maintain a frank and open approach.

There are a number of practical considerations to be observed when an interview is conducted. If an interview is one of a series, set the scene and summarise what has happened previously at other interviews. Pace it in relation to the time available, which should be identified at the start. One hour is about right, and it is difficult to retain attention and concentration if the time taken exceeds 90 minutes. Try to ensure that interruptions are minimised, for these can make it very difficult to develop an interview in a structured way and, if very intrusive, can make it a waste of time. Ensure messages or calls for you do not disrupt the interview. If possible hold the interview at the interviewee's work place, for this will enable useful background information on the working environment to be collected. Make sure all the areas and items in your interview plan are covered in the course of the interview, but do not do this in a way which inhibits the interviewee's flow of dialogue. Always be prepared to vary the plan if circumstances show this to be necessary. It is a good idea though, to contain discussion at any one time within one of the discrete areas identified in the interview plan. If the interviewee wanders too far from the point discussion must be refocused. Often this can be done by use of a clarifying summary of the part of the interview immediately preceding, which is followed up with a question that seeks to redirect discussion to where the interviewer wants to be. The interviewer must try to remain in control. It is generally best to ask open questions, for example 'could you explain your understanding of this issue?' Ask as few questions as possible which encourage 'yes' and 'no' answers. Avoid leading questions. These can be of several types, for example ones which convey to the interviewee that the interviewer is seeking a particular response, or those which, in the circumstances that prevail, have an obvious answer with which the interviewee is likely to go along, regardless of personal views. Advice about the phrasing of questions can only be given in general terms, and there may be occasions when closed questions are necessary, or a straight 'yes' or 'no' answer is required. The point to remember is that the interviewer should use question types in a deliberate and planned way. The tone of voice used when a question is put can also inhibit a free reply.

Notes may be taken in various ways and should suit the personal preference of the interviewer, but must be comprehensible afterwards. Some form of personal shorthand is usually necessary if note taking is not to interfere with the flow of the interview. If there are two people available one of them can take the notes, but in such a situation someone should clearly take the lead. Unless this is done the opportunity to build a structured interview based on an interview plan is lost. Interview by committee rarely works, and it is normally undesirable for more than two people to visit an interviewee. It is polite to ask the interviewee for permission to take notes.

At the end of the interview attempt to withdraw in such a way that the interviewee can be re-approached for further information or clarification, if this becomes necessary. Always finish on amicable terms. Make sure the interviewee is thanked for the time given up and the contribution made. If the interviewee makes any observations or asks for specific feedback deal seriously with the points raised and, if possible, comply with them. If direct response is not possible, say so, and why that is the case.

After the interview is over attach the date of the interview to the notes taken and the name or names of those involved. How far notes are developed into a formal transcript depends on the needs of the situation and personal preference. Unless it is essential to insert them in the final report, or they may be disputed, there is no need to produce a mutually agreed draft. Notes should however be put in a state that is intelligible to the note taker after a period of time has elapsed, or to someone else who becomes involved in the assignment, and needs to acquire a detailed knowledge of work completed so far.

3 Using statistical techniques effectively

The application of statistical techniques can be very beneficial, provided the base data is accurate, and there are precise and reasonably predictable units available within which to aggregate the data. Such techniques are particularly applicable to the analysis of large amounts of factual data. However, as with many techniques, there are potential dangers as well as benefits. It is very important to be aware of them. Ensure the technique used matches the circumstances, for it is quite possible, if this is not the case, to produce precise but useless analyses. Use statistical techniques as aids to better understanding, and appreciate that they cannot be substituted for judgement. A danger of over-reliance on statistical information is that it 'takes over', and ends up in control of an organisation instead of being a support to effective management.

4 Statistical analysis

The main purpose of using statistical techniques in assignment work is to define and to quantify the current situation. The choice of technique depends on the nature of the data and the needs of the person for whom the work is undertaken. There are a wide range of techniques to choose from, for example activity sampling, calculation of distributions. The great value of statistical techniques is that they aid clear and precise presentation of an issue. Several examples are illustrated in figure 2.

Data may be collected on the basis of two principles: measure everything, or take samples. The following three questions need to be answered in deciding which method to use:

- is the data static? ie not constantly changing,
- is the amount of data large?
- how accurate must the results be?

The final decision on whether to count everything or take samples must also take account of the costs involved in using one or other method, and the objectives of the study. If a high degree of accuracy is necessary it is more likely that the 'measure all' approach is appropriate. If accuracy is not essential sampling is more convenient. Sampling can give results within determined confidence limits, ie how many times out of a hundred the obtained figure will be right, and the answer is usually in the form of a range, for example plus or minus five units, or per cent, as appropriate.

The data collected for analysis of current situations can also be used to project or predict future needs, demands or results. The main methods are of two types; simple or complex. Techniques in the simple group are basically ways of predicting future results, eg trend curves and graphs, time series analyses, and rise and fall graphs based on patterns observed in the current data, but adjusted to take account of foreseen changes in circumstances. They can be used without expert help and can be applied manually or with the aid of a statistical calculator. Complex applications usually involve computer analysis, and probably reference to an appropriate expert, as would be necessary in the use of linear programming or regression analysis.

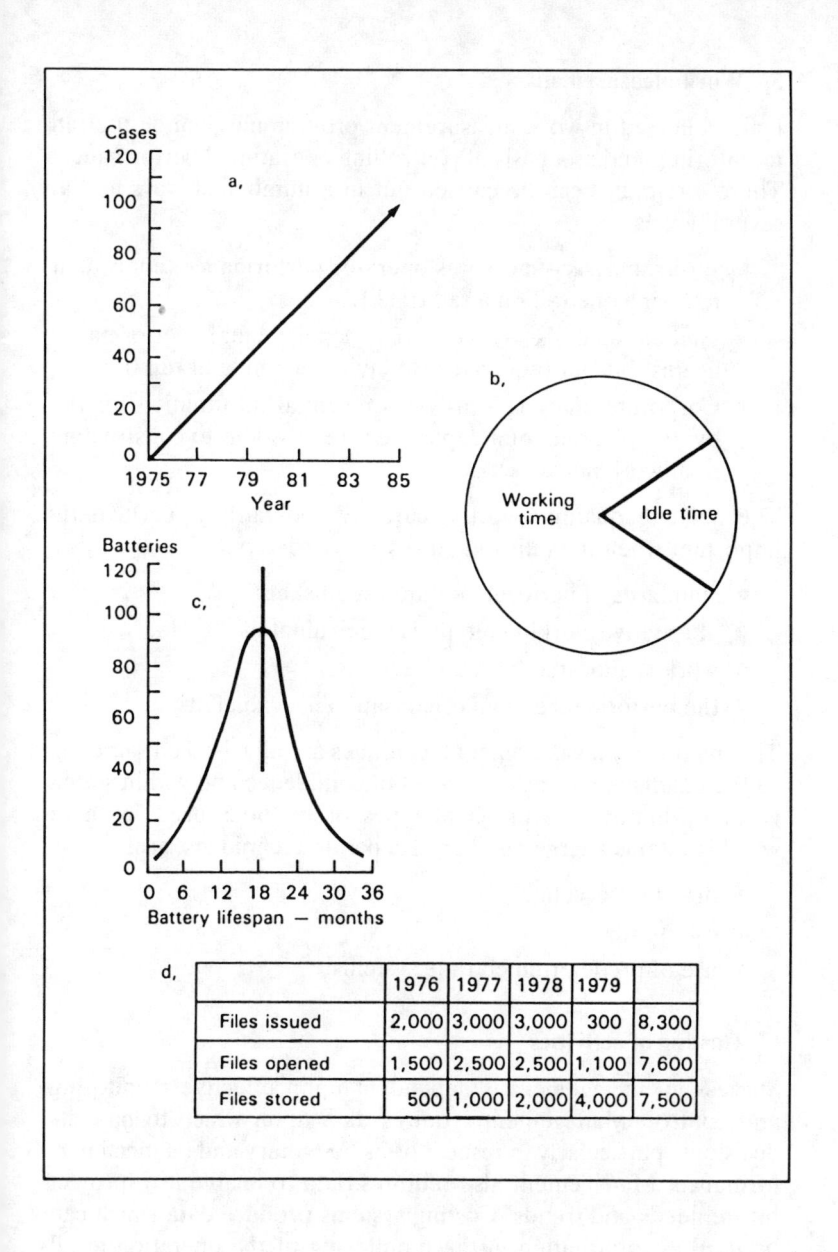

Figure 2 **Examples of the use of statistical techniques to provide information**

5 Work measurement

Data collected in work measurement programmes can be used in monitoring, and as a basis of controlling operational performance. These disciplines can be carried out in a number of ways and at several levels.

- Basic analysis – measures operator performance (equivalent to laying one rail on a rail track).
- Higher analysis – measures departmental performance against budget (equivalent to laying one mile of rail track).
- Corporate analysis – provides essential information for the overall planning of a department (equivalent to constructing a railwork network).

The need to quantify work accurately and fairly is particularly important when the following tasks are carried out:

- standards of performance are established;
- alternative working methods are evaluated;
- work is allocated between sections;
- the performance of an organisation is evaluated.

The main work measurement techniques are all based on sampling so the results are always to a level of confidence and within stated accuracy limits. The principal types of methods used, each of which contains a large number of separate techniques, are:

- direct observation;
- estimating;
- use of predetermined time systems.

6 Costing of activities

Success in management is dependent upon effective monitoring and control. Management requires data upon which to base its decisions, particularly in respect of its budgetary and financial performance. Management also requires data to enable it to project future needs and trends. Costing systems produce data which can be used as information in the monitoring of the operation at all levels.

There are a large number of costing systems or techniques, all developed to satisfy specific needs or situations. The technique to use is determined by,

- the level at which control is desired;
- the use to be made of the data; and
- the degree and nature of interlinkage with other management systems.

Costing methods can vary from the very simple to the extremely complex. One of the most commonly applied systems is standard or unit costing which is most easily applicable where units of output are identifiable and reasonably easily measured. The aim is to produce a standard cost for processing one unit of output. The standard is set after:

- identifying all areas of cost that should be included; and
- deciding an output level on which the standard is to be based.

Simplified costing can be applied to areas of work where simple and precise identification and measurement of work units is not possible. Its purpose is to describe and quantify representative expenditure in any one year. Only grossed up figures are used and only two elements are taken into account; capital and operating costs.

A standard cost is used as a yardstick against which to compare the actual performance of a single unit, which may be a department, office, or even an individual person. Constituent elements from within standard and actual cost data can be used as the means of investigating performance variances from the standard. Simplified costings can also provide a mechanism for monitoring actual expenditure against that planned, but in a broad brush way. Cost data can be made the basis for other types of monitoring, most usually in association with budgetary systems. Cost data can also be a major source of information in the determination of budgets, and although a budget does not have to be based on cost data, it is much more likely to be meaningful if this is the case.

Both costing and budgetary systems are used in projecting future requirements or demands. The impact of changes to unit costs and the effect this has on performance can be estimated in relation to the various constituent elements, ie costs, volumes, or quantities of the units involved. This can help management to decide priority between options. In the budgetary context indications of future requirements for manpower, training, or any other item of expenditure, can be obtained by application of the projection techniques already described to existing data. Costing and budgetary information provide background intelligence for decision making and help to monitor performance.

7 Costing of proposals

This is essential in all assignments, although costs and savings may not be the only factor to be taken into account when making recommendations. Costing in this context has two aspects. One is the costing of existing operations and the second is costing of new proposals so that comparisons can be made. The technique can also be used to help decide between several alternative potential courses of action. Two methods are particularly useful for costing proposals, namely unit and simplified costing.

8 Forms design

A well designed form reflects the needs of the user and the originator to ensure that the information conveyed can be:

- understood easily;
- used effectively.

A form that does not meet the above requirements incurs penalties which arise from error rates. These may lead to a substantial amount of additional time being spent on queries, and result in higher marginal costs.

Before starting the process of design the analyst, whether a forms specialist, or a management services assignment officer, should be convinced that:

- the form is really necessary;
- there is no other form serving the same purpose; and
- the proposed form cannot sensibly be combined with one which already exists.

9 Operational research

Operational research is the application of scientific methods to complex problems of management. The technique involves the use of mathematical modelling as a substitute for practical experimentation where this is not possible, because of complexity of circumstance or impracticality. The mathematical model incorporates factors such as chance and risk and compares outcomes using alternative decision processes, strategies and controls. Operational research is most useful where management has a clear need to make objective decisions but cannot afford, or has not time or opportunity, to undertake practical experiments. Its findings are reliable within the parameters of uncertainty specified.

10 Charting the work

Flow charting describes in detail current or proposed systems and procedures in graphical form. There are a number of different systems in general use. The technique is particularly useful when the work under investigation is too complicated for the details to be retained in the memory. The charting of procedures can be very useful as a synoptic analysis contributing to the overall simplification of the practices involved, and as a way of formally documenting them in a report.

Project network technique is a planning and control system which shows graphically the relationships and dependencies between a number of tasks within a project. A network of activities is constructed and the durations of each task added. From this process the overall duration of the project is derived and the longest path through the network identified. This is the 'critical path', and represents the set of dependent activities that must be controlled and managed if the overall project is to be delivered on time. The logic of the network and the activity timings should be kept under regular review. Activities not on the critical path will have spare capacity, or 'float', which may be used to support the critical path activities. This technique is appropriate to the analysis of both small and large scale projects. It can be used to aid efficient planning of a management services assignment, or to help unravel all the component parts in the activities being studied. It helps to identify what are the key elements in a complex process, and the same principles can be applied through the use of a computer.

11 Creative thinking

The analytical methods described in this book are mostly 'logical' in type, because the principles of rational analysis that they employ are very effective in the solution of practical problems. There are however, other ways of helping to find solutions to problems, which are collectively known as 'creative thinking'. They all involve making imaginative leaps from one situation or idea to another. The differences which exist between the two approaches should not be exaggerated for both ought to contain elements of the other. For example it is quite common to have moments of illumination during the course of 'logical' analysis that could be described as 'creative thinking'.

There is though a special place for the formal use of creative thinking. Sometimes our usual reasoning methods prove unequal to the task and an impass is reached however much effort is made. Something different is required to break the mould and a special effort has to be made to generate ideas. Brainstorming is often thought of as a technique to apply in such a situation, but although it is very useful an organised group of people is necessary to produce meaningful results. Many books have been written on brainstorming and reference should be made to them to obtain more information on how it is practiced.

There are other methods of creative thinking that are easier to apply and can be used by individuals in an informal way. A few, mentioned below, can be applied by assignment officers at any appropriate time during an assignment.

- List the main features or characteristics of an activity or object, followed by an examination of each to see how it can be changed and improved. This method is particularly useful where basic component parts of an activity or object operate discretely and can be relatively easily identified, eg the way a form is distributed, completed and acted on.
- Force ideas or objects together that are currently not closely related and assess the potential outcome. This practice works

well with intangible issues and can help organisational analysis.

- Make checklists or aides memoire as pointers to ideas, or to prevent ideas being forgotten.

All forms of creative thinking have a characteristic working procedure:

Preparation. Make sure all the relevant background information is available and understood.

Suspension of criticism. Set aside traditional critical judgements. It is necessary to be prepared to take into account the most outlandish ideas, and to appraise genuinely their possible usefulness. Such willingness is necessary to ensure a complete break is secured from the previously unproductive way of thinking.

Generation of ideas. Many ideas are required and the emphasis is on quantity not quality. They do not have to be logical or practical. Many of the ideas produced will be of no use, but often only one good one is needed! This stage can be frustrating and seem pointless but it is an essential part of the method.

Incubation. Ideas need time to be considered in the mind, sometimes at a subconscious level. This stage is equivalent to 'sleeping' on a problem and should not be forced along too quickly.

Perception. There comes a possible moment when one, or several, of the ideas produced is seen to be of help in solving the problem.

Refinement. Final judgement has to be made on how the good idea needs to be developed to be of practical assistance.

CHAPTER VI: FORMULATING THE PROPOSALS AND SEEKING AGREEMENT

1 The heart of the assignment

For the sake of clarity distinct chronological divisions have been made between analysis, diagnosis, and the formulation of proposals, but in reality these divisions will probably not occur so neatly. It is likely that some proposals will emerge during the completion of background work and even be implemented immediately to get early benefit. But ideas about solutions will be further developed during analysis and diagnosis, either by the assignment officer, the client, or during joint discussion. There eventually comes a stage in an assignment when overall proposals have to be given firm shape, and hard decisions made between possible alternative courses of action. This is the process now discussed and the discipline it involves is inevitable if clear-cut final recommendations are to emerge.

The aim should be to develop firm recommendations for the client. This is not always easy. When several options appear to have equal value one method of approach is to put them forward as alternatives, from which a final decision can be made on the action to be taken. Such a practice should never be resorted to by the assignment officer as a device to pass difficult choices to the client, and should only be used when there are genuine alternatives to be considered. If it is thought it may be necessary to present options, the strategy to be followed in their formulation should be established at the contract phase of the assignment.

2 Formulating the proposals

The process of analysis and diagnosis should result in overall conclusions being reached about how the issues or problems involved are best resolved. The formulation of proposals puts the diagnosis into a structured form that has practical application. The five diagnostic tests outlined earlier (see section 4 of chapter IV) should help considerably in deciding what proposals to make.

It is very important that proposals are objectively derived from the evidence. If ideas do not fit with the information collected they must be discarded, since otherwise faulty proposals could be adopted. It is easier to ignore factual evidence than is often realised. There are two main reasons why this happens. The first stems from over-attachment to ideas which simply do not fit the evidence. If an idea is held very strongly, facts which show it to be partly or wholly wrong, are easily ignored. The second is external pressure, either direct or assumed. Assignment staff themselves may be tempted not to raise issues because it is believed they will be offensive to powerful interested parties, or because they will offend too strongly against conventional wisdom. Objectives should be reviewed regularly to ensure that they meet the current needs of the organisation.

In straightforward assignments proposals often flow logically from the analytical and diagnostic work, when fully and rigorously completed. In more complex assignments proposals may not be derived so easily; for instance, where a number of options present themselves the final choice can be very difficult, particularly when judgements are required on intangible factors. In such situations factual analysis, for example costing, can only be of ancillary help. Examples of intangible factors which can be an important influence in assignments are listed below.

Reaction of the client and staff affected. This can be conditioned by a wide range of considerations, for example need to balance costs against acceptability to staff when alternative computer systems are appraised, or the difficulty in choosing between various possible ways of providing a public service.

Policy decisions and social considerations. These may demand immediate response, or require to be considered in terms of likely future impact.

The rate of development and implementation of information technology. Cost trends can change over time, for example costs of electronic equipment tend to decline rapidly as usage widens and design and manufacture are refined. Decisions concerning the introduction of change into an organisation may require the anticipation of such trends.

In evaluating these, and other intangible factors, the assignment officer can find it helpful to draw on central Civil Service or departmental specialist advice. Such help should, however, be considered with care, as it is likely to be general rather than specific and may not be fully applicable to the detailed issues at hand. It may be necessary to refer to senior assignment staff, particularly if manpower, training, accommodation, or other resource matters are of major significance. The fact that difficult judgements are usually required about important issues, serves to reinforce the need to avoid errors and take advice. Inexperienced assignment officers faced with difficult decisions should be especially aware that the ability to make good judgements develops over time, and be prepared to seek guidance from an experienced practitioner whose professional view they respect. Interested parties are most likely to have firm views of their own about important problems and seek to exert pressure in their resolution.

There is one aim that must underlie all others when formulating proposals, namely that specific recommendations secure improved efficiency or effectiveness, or both. The gains should be quantified whenever possible, especially if additional overall costs will be incurred. Not all recommendations can be justified in this way, and none should be set aside just because their benefits are unquantifiable.

3 Seeking agreement: the basic approach

Emphasis has already been placed on the importance of developing proposals and ideas in a participative manner, so that line management and staff become involved in an investigation and contribute their ideas. Ideally client 'ownership' of emerging proposals should be promoted. Clearly this process needs to start right at the beginning of an assignment, and should certainly not be commenced suddenly when formal proposals are developed. Consultation should flow naturally throughout the life of an assignment.

The assignment officer's prime concern is to devise constructive, relevant, and beneficial proposals, and to get them implemented. The general approach to assignment completion should be one that fosters these ends. If line management is encouraged to contribute early on in the investigation this is likely to result in more pertinent recommendations, and to lead to a positive approach to implementation. It is an important part of the assignment officer's role to promote these attitudes among line management, for if they are absent it is unlikely that implementation will be pursued with vigour.

4 Clinching an agreement

However an assignment has progressed there inevitably comes a time when formal recommendations have to be agreed. The responsibility for securing a positive outcome is shared between the assignment staff and the client. The assignment staff must devise clear proposals, whether they consist of one recommendation or several options. Assignment staff should emphasise the positive gains to be made from proposals, and if reference to past or current practice is necessary, care should be taken to avoid doing this disparagingly. The process involved in the conclusion of an agreement requires the ability to negotiate and sell, and a flexible approach. Agreement on the principal issues should not be risked by pushing too hard for acceptance of less essential matters. It is important to have a very clear idea of objectives and essential issues, and to be flexible in their achievement.

Usually a report is produced in which is contained a review of the work completed, together with the conclusions reached and the recommendations made. The content of this is sometimes presented verbally before the written version is finished. The report will probably take a while to write and is best done in consultation with the assignment officer's own manager and client. It is then possible to resolve problem issues, or misunderstandings, fairly easily, and the process of securing agreement remains a continuous shared process to the end. The situation must be avoided where a report, produced without consultation, is presented to an unprepared client at a formal presentation session. With this proviso there is no set or ideal way for the presentation of recommendations. In contrast to reliance on the written report, it is possible for it to be done almost entirely by verbal means, together with only a brief written summary of the main points. Sometimes it is sensible to present the preliminary report verbally and then write up the outcome of that meeting in a formal way. It is also possible, in circumstances where the client already knows and accepts the results of the survey, to dispense with a formal presentation session unless it is required for a specific purpose. The proposals may, for instance, need public demonstration, or it is important to convey the principles of the proposals to a wider audience. Whatever method is used some form of written statement is advisable to document the outcome of the investigation, to provide a record of what has occurred.

The situation sometimes arises where although no difficulty is encountered in the agreement of the main recommendations, it is not easy to secure understanding about important areas of detail. This can happen in large projects when the various parties involved do not understand fully how the detailed elements link together, or when it is impossible to resolve such questions without testing ideas in practice. In such circumstances follow-up discussions between assignment staff and the client may be necessary. It may even be desirable for assignment staff to assist in the testing of recommendations in order to establish the best way to proceed.

If, notwithstanding every effort to reach agreement this proves impossible, the assignment staff's proposals should not be withdrawn without good reason. The existence of serious doubts about the validity of proposals may make it necessary to retest or re-evaluate them. This provides opportunity either to convince management of their appropriateness, or to make modifications that are required. If, after such a reappraisal has been made, management still refuses to accept the proposals, assignment staff should stand firm as long as they are convinced of the correctness of their position. No good will come of agreeing to implement inadequate proposals. A firm stand may in the end lead to acceptance, and failing this, it does no harm for proposals to 'lie on the table' for a while. Many reports have been implemented at a later date after a period of reflection by those concerned. Sound recommendations are often taken up by senior line management even though they are rejected at the time of presentation.

CHAPTER VII: COMMUNICATING THE FINDINGS

1 Purpose

This book has stressed the importance of establishing and maintaining a positive relationship with the client throughout an assignment. If this is done effectively it is possible to avoid much of the tension that can be associated with the formal presentation of findings, because there will be nothing of substance in them that has not been accepted informally already. This ideal cannot always be achieved, and some assignments are imposed by top management, but, whatever the situation, the client should always have some knowledge of final proposals before a formal outline is received. Only if very special circumstances exist, which make it impossible to adopt an open approach, is it right to develop proposals in isolation of the client. The final communication of findings should round off the assignment in a way that is satisfactory to all those involved. However this is done the prime objective should be to sell proposals positively and get them implemented.

There are two principal forms of presentation. Traditionally, the written report has been the main one, but there is a growing tendency to supplement this with a verbal presentation, often as a precursor to its completion. This practice helps to speed up the acceptance of recommendations, ensures recommendations are not placed with the client without warning, and provides a natural conclusion to the joint development of proposals with the client.

2 The written report

There are two purposes in preparing a report; first to record the results of the enquiry and document it, and secondly, to present the findings in such a way that acceptance and implementation of the recommendations is enhanced. If the second of these objectives is to be achieved the report needs to be presented in the way that is most useful to the client, which means that wide variations in layout and content are to be expected. If an assignment, for example, recommends a simple change in office procedure or limited mechanisation, the report may consist of no more than explanatory charts and diagrams with a note of agreed action accompanied by a simple covering letter. But if the assignment recommendations require senior management's consideration, and the issues involved are complex, a more formal and extensive report will most likely be necessary. Even then the main sections should be kept brief, with the bulk of the supporting material confined to cross referenced appendices. A summary of the findings and recommendations at the beginning helps those reading it to focus on the main issues, and if the report is a large one it may also be sensible to accompany this with a synopsis. Assignment staff need to consider the report's content and plan, in relation to client needs, at an early stage in its preparation. Drafts should be reviewed as the writing proceeds, particularly in terms of content, presentation and style. The completion of each draft is obviously a useful point to do this.

There are no overall or binding rules concerning the structure of a report, because the primary need is for it to be pertinent to the circumstances and issues addressed. Brevity and clarity however need to be the guiding principles. The following framework is suggested, to be used whenever possible. Set report structures exist in some departments and, where they are used, the advice given here will have to be modified to accommodate their requirements.

Title page and list of contents.

Introduction. This provides background and outlines the objectives of the report. Acknowledgements should be stated.

Summary of findings, conclusions and recommendations. Sometimes a brief synopsis is added if the report is large.

Body of report. This should deal directly with the main points and how these, and the conclusions, have been derived from the information analysed. It should not contain detailed supporting documentation. In putting forward the proposals attention should be focused on the likely changes that will result from their implementation. It is also important to insert an outline of the arrangements for dealing with implementation and follow up, normally through an agreed 'action plan'.

Statement of recommendations. Express these briefly and with clarity. Cross references should be included to the appropriate paragraphs in the main report or appendices, where their justification and supporting detail is documented.

Appendices. This section of the report is not to be treated as equivalent to a rubbish bin for factual information that cannot be fitted in elsewhere in the report. Information contained in it should not be thrown together, but presented with care. One of the main objectives of a report is to support implementation, and the appendices are where people go to find the justification for arguments made elsewhere. Every effort therefore needs to be made to maximise impact by the use of clear tables, graphs and charts etc. Appendices should be cross referenced to specific sections in the body of the report.

Some people find the preparation of a draft report the most difficult part of the assignment, and few have perfect drafting skills. It is usual to draw up several versions or outlines, each being nearer to the final product than the one before. In the initial draft do not bother too much about style, and concentrate on ensuring that the main points are made logically and clearly within the overall framework adopted. Once the logical order of the points has been established effort can be concentrated in later drafts on polishing the presentation. There are two main aspects to this; ensure that points or arguments are stated simply and clearly, and keep the overall report as concise as possible. The use of simple words and short sentences is an invaluable aid to achieving this successfully. A word processor can be a help in editing and amending drafts, and saves time. As soon as the assignment officer believes the draft to be in reasonable shape the comments of other people should be obtained. Those involved with the assignment can comment mainly on content and presentation, while outsiders can be asked to comment on general impact and presentation. If the preparation of a draft is approached in a disciplined way it should not be too difficult to produce an acceptable report. Table 4 (overleaf) contains a checklist of points which assist in maintaining the self-discipline required. They are not necessarily in order of importance.

Submission should not be delayed since reports can quickly become outdated, and failure to build conclusively on the work completed during the course of an assignment can lead to loss of impetus and interest. The report is submitted to the person who

Table 4 **Checklist to aid report writing**

a. Plan the report in outline before starting to write.
b. Maintain a neutral and unemotive style appropriate to an advisor.
c. Use short sentences and state arguments simply and clearly.
d. Use terms familiar to the client but ensure they are intelligible to others.
e. Use terms consistently, and define them at the beginning.
f. Refer to posts by title.
g. Arrange paragraphs within a section so that there is a natural and sequential development of argument.
h. Avoid jargon and repetitive standard phrases.
i. Explain the point of appendices, and ensure they are fully cross referenced to other parts of the report.
j. Avoid overstatement or generalisation beyond what is strictly justified.
k. Thank those who have helped you.

commissioned it, usually with a covering letter expressing thanks and any other comments necessary. These may include a statement of points which are significant but cannot be inserted in the formal document. The assignment officer should obtain from the client a statement of how many copies will be required, and ensure a sufficient quantity is available by the issue date. Above all the assignment officer should ensure the report is well typed, reproduced and packaged.

3 The verbal report

The objective of a verbal report is to complement the formal written document. It does this in two ways; by helping to sell the proposals and also to save time. These benefits are obtained through the face to face contact involved. It provides the opportunity to come to a quick, but not forced, decision about implementation, and is a good vehicle for identifying precisely any problems likely to hold back acceptance and implementation. A verbal presentation is much more immediate than a written report, and there is less opportunity for misunderstanding and confusion to arise. The written report is not always the best means for obtaining a decision and can lead to delay. However the verbal presentation does not remove the need for a formal report, which is still required as a record of the investigation. The information it contains may be very important during the implementation stage.

The structure of a verbal presentation needs to be tailored, just as much as in a written report, to take account of the complexity of the assignment and the needs of the client. But there are some influences which are specific to verbal reporting. The type of audience – senior management, middle management, junior management or clerical – will determine the content. Presentations to senior management ought to concentrate on why the proposals are necessary, and those to clerical staff on how they are to be achieved. Between these types of audience there can be a varying mixture of requirement. The exact need will vary in each individual situation, depending on how the work is organised, but usually the higher the level of staff involved the more emphasis needs to be put on explanation, and the more junior they are the more emphasis is required on how the changes are to work.

The objectives of a presentation will also vary in relation to the type of audience involved. A presentation to senior management is concerned to gain acceptance; to middle management to obtain commitment and explain how the changes will work; and at the junior levels to clarify implementation in such a way as to promote commitment.

Even though presentations differ in content and objectives there is always a common framework that can be used as a model. It comprises:

Introduction. Outline the purpose of the presentation, make the opening impact and provide the foundation on which the rest of the presentation is based.

Body of presentation. Outline present work situation and practices, the analysis of findings and proposals made.

Conclusion. Outline again the proposals and their justification, state the benefits that will be obtained, the costs involved, and date of implementation. Make a powerful ending.

Questions.

The preparation of a verbal report can be commenced by making an outline in the same way as suggested for a written report, but in fleshing it out there are important differences. A presentation forces the presenter to be more selective about the information provided, since all the detail cannot be included. The selection of material must be based very precisely on the audience to be addressed and the desired objective. Choices need to be made between what material is essential, what is useful, and what can be left out within the time allowed. Once these decisions have been made attention can be turned to the actual means of presentation taking account of constraints which exist – particularly the time available, the location, and the time of day the presentation will be made. Visual communication should be maximised, since there is an appreciably higher retention rate for information so presented.

A positive impact is essential if maximum benefit is to be obtained from a verbal presentation. Presenters must be competent at putting their material over. The potential strength of the verbal report is that it helps to make decisions more quickly, but there are also dangers associated with it. If a presentation fails to make a positive impact, or leaves an audience confused, proposals may be rejected without good reason, or doubts be unnecessarily raised as to the worth of the recommendations. In such a situation a great deal of assignment effort may be put at risk which can only be retrieved by further work and effort to rebuild confidence. Observance of the points outlined in Table 5 should help to guard against negative response.

Table 5 **Points to remember when making a verbal presentation**

a. Catch and hold interest early in the presentation.

b. Repeat the main points several times.

c. Make sure the objectives and content are correct for the type of audience addressed.

d. Make sure conclusions are fully justified and that they emerge clearly from the analysis of the problems.

e. Rehearse the presentation.

f. Try to get a favourable venue and time of day for the presentation – away from the client's office and mid-morning are ideal.

g. Always remember the presenter's personal impact is very important.

h. Check the equipment to be used in the presentation works.

i. Ensure visual aids are clear, and contain the minimum amount of information to make the point intended.

CHAPTER VIII: IMPLEMENTATION

1 The importance of effective implementation

It has been accepted traditionally that line management, or the sponsor if different, is solely responsible for implementation. Often an assignment finished with the formal presentation of a report and any further involvement was usually limited to a routine follow-up after six months. This way of working has provided opportunity for implementation to be put off, or abandoned. If a report is left unimplemented for a long period the claim can be made that its recommendations have been overtaken by events. The increased emphasis now being placed on planning is intended to prevent these occurrences.

There are a variety of reasons why line management fails to take action on recommendations. It may have become convinced, perhaps wrongly, that there has been a change in need or objectives since the proposals were made which make them wholly or partly irrelevant. Line management may also find difficulty in implementing the recommendations and become convinced that they are unimplementable, which may of course be true. The development of staff problems at the beginning or during the course of implementation can also cause delay. Such problems sometimes occur naturally, for example when there are losses of suitably trained and qualified people, or as the result of pressure for general staff economies. These types of problems encourage inaction when line management does not fully understand what has to be done to bring implementation about.

2 Responsibility for implementation

Effective implementation of recommendations is made more likely if the parties involved are clear about their individual responsibilities for achieving it. An important issue in this context is to what extent, if at all, assignment staff should 'hand-hold' line management. There are two practical issues to be considered.

- The extent to which the assignment officer should be responsible for securing the agreement and implementation of proposals.
- The extent to which the assignment officer should be available to help with implementation.

It must always be clearly understood that management is wholly responsible for implementation. A more formal involvement by management services' personnel could lead to misunderstandings, and provoke the charge that management's role is being usurped. To guard against this happening, assignment staff must be clear about their role, which is to advise and support management, and be sure they are only seen to contribute in this way.

There is one other set of responsibilities to be noted, and it is of considerable importance. The ultimate client is generally senior line management, or even top management, and it is crucial that they actively support the implementation of recommendations. It is also important that all those affected by the assignment know of this support. Progress in implementation should be relayed regularly to senior and top management.

3 Planning implementation

The clear identification of roles and responsibilities for line management and assignment staff is a basic pre-requisite for the planning of implementation. It is wise to plan for implementation at the earliest practicable stage. Even though line management is responsible for implementation there remains a clear role for the assignment officer who can act as helper, counsellor and sounding board and fulfil three clear-cut functions throughout implementation.

- Be available and, if the process is complex, be ready to assist.
- Help to monitor the application of proposals and sort out difficulties, if it is not necessary to be more actively involved.
- Be available to help train those who will be taking on new roles as the proposals are applied.

This division and allocation of responsibilities should help provide the basis for the creation of an action plan, which should be seen as an integral part of the assignment. Planning for implementation should begin as soon as firm proposals are developed, and certainly before these are formally presented. The action plan should be included in final proposals and form part of the written or verbal report. It should subsequently be the central reference and guide to the implementation process as a whole. Because of its importance the action plan needs to be drawn up in conjunction with, and be acceptable to, line management since line management is going to have the main responsibility for making it work. The action plan for implementation needs to include the following detailed points.

- A timetable for implementation, with a completion date.
- The line management's specific responsibilities.
- The assignment officer's specific responsibilities.
- A date on which the assignment officer's support will end.
- Checkpoints on progress, with dates, for reporting progress to senior and top management.
- The training plan for staff affected.

Emphasis has been placed in this book on constructive planning to bring about change, which needs to be a continuous concern throughout an assignment. It is essential that the specification of an action plan for implementation is seen as part of the overall process of planning for change. A positive attitude by line management to implementation is highly desirable, and their views can be profoundly affected by the assignment officer's approach throughout the assignment, whose importance in this context has been discussed earlier. It will not be elaborated on here, except to stress that the plan for implementation is likely to be more effective if it is built on a positive and outgoing approach towards the client.

4 Training

Training needs raised by the assignment have to be recognised, and provision made for them to be met. People affected by significant change cannot be expected to meet the demands of the new situation without some help, and in any case, training is an excellent way to promote acceptance of new ideas and confidence in making them work. If a training officer is not available to plan the training with assistance from the assignment officer, the assignment officer should do it personally. There is a basic requirement for the training needs of the people who will be affected by the proposed changes to be identified, and for a training programme to be prepared. This may be elaborate if the project is complex and several different jobs and posts are affected. It may be necessary to train initially a small group of people who then train a bigger group, or for people to be trained at differing levels of understanding. The assignment officer should play an active part in the identification of the need and in early training activity, but then withdraw on a planned basis. Every opportunity should be taken to involve some of those affected by the proposals in the training process, particularly the manager of the activity concerned.

5 Withdrawal of the assignment officer

During implementation a major concern of the assignment officer is to ensure line management does not come to be too dependent on the assistance provided. Indeed it should be the objective of the assignment officer to see that assistance is progressively reduced on a planned basis, so this does not happen. Any involvement of an assignment officer in implementation should be for a limited period which, ideally, is stated specifically in the implementation plan. Exactly what assistance should be given will depend on a variety of factors; the needs of the line manager, the general availability of assignment staff, local traditions, and the circumstances prevailing at the time.

If serious problems or difficulties arise during implementation special action may need to be taken. Further testing may be required, or if fundamental doubts about the recommendations arise, a review may be necessary. Senior management representatives, both from management services and the line activity should always be involved in such circumstances.

CHAPTER IX: APPLYING INFORMATION TECHNOLOGY

1 The main issues

Why have a specific chapter on this subject? After all the principles on which assignment work is based, the primary concern of this book, apply in all circumstances. The justification for making a special case of information technology rests on two grounds. One is the overwhelming impact, in scale and extent, of developments in information technology now taking place, and likely to occur in future years. They will penetrate most people's daily working lives to a greater degree than previous computer based developments. In addition this technology will promote new approaches to work. Profound changes in the way work is carried out may often be possible, particularly in relation to its organisation and the need for it.

The variety and range of facilities are increasing and less skill is required to use them. It is now possible to obtain data almost instantly and in ways which meet specific needs. This is possible because of the convergence of technology, particularly through the combination of computing power with the keyboard to provide word processing capability, and the ability to access information remotely through telecommunications links. How easy it is in practice to organise and harness these technological developments will have a major influence on the character and speed of application.

Success in optimising the use of information technology is complicated by the high rate at which technological innovation occurs. This causes problems in managing the introduction of information technology, and prompts managers to be cautious in their approach to it. Successful exploitation will also be influenced by the degree to which information technology strategies are identified and implemented in support of overall objectives. Without a framework of this type it is difficult to gain value from money spent. Moreover, if information technology is applied in a haphazard way a reaction against it can easily develop. Two further issues are influencing the wider use of information technology. The requirement to observe statutory provisions for the protection of privacy can be restrictive, as can the need to maintain confidentiality within the organisation. Progress in design and reliability, of both software and equipment, will also influence the degree to which information technology penetrates organisational life. Because technological developments have been so rapid and widespread there is a tendency to overlook potential limitations stemming from this area. Reliability of computers can still present problems. Failure to achieve design improvements which will make equipment more acceptable and easy to operate, may prevent the universal application that some experts predict. At present use of the keyboard, a piece of equipment that is not accepted easily by everyone, is unavoidable and it may not be technically possible to do away with it entirely.

The implications of developments in information technology for the content and organisation of work are unclear. Jobs wholly related to the technology itself will be changed drastically, or cease to exist, but there are relatively few that are of this type. In most instances the impact will be partial or even marginal. This may lead to a reduction in the numbers of jobs required in certain work areas, but the removal of part of a job may encourage more weight to be given to other aspects which previously received insufficient attention. Some new tasks will be created by the technology itself, and new specialist jobs will emerge. It is likely that major reorganisation will occur where very clear gains in the quality or quantity of services provided can be obtained, and there is popular pressure for the changes to be made. Where pressures are less strong, and the gains less clear, rationalisation may be slow to be achieved. Increased flexibility in job working will almost certainly be promoted, which will have implications for job definition and grading, particularly at junior levels.

One of the principal impacts stemming from these developments is increased flexibility in applying the technology. It is now much easier to meet the needs of specific situations, because of the more widespread availability of pre-programmed packages, and the increased availability of microcomputers and computer terminals. Complex applications can be catered for too, although they may need to be tailormade. Projects can be very large or quite small, but they will nearly always arise at the request of line management and will operate under their control. Although assignment officers will assist in design and application, their role will tend to be different from that in many previous types of computer application, because of the more direct responsibility exercised by line management.

In these circumstances the appraisal of project viability will be extremely important, and become a significant task for assignment staff. It may well be more difficult to justify individual proposals because of the need to make careful examination of local circumstances, and to ensure conformity with wider strategies is maintained. The development of having less direct control, combined with the need to have detailed understanding in order to define and quantify gains will complicate the management services role. It goes without saying that the need to plan will grow in importance. One of the great difficulties with the application of office technology, particularly in the ways described here, is actually to quantify the promised benefits and realise them. This can arise for a number of reasons: the foreseen benefits may be overestimated; it may be difficult to gain agreement on economical operation; or capital and related costs get stated or projected inaccurately. Changes in work requirements or developments in technology during a project can complicate the process of both quantification and realisation of benefits.

The application of information technology has other, wider implications for assignment staff. Assignments are more likely to require overall appraisal of line management needs, as opposed to assessment of specific and specialist processes. The volume of advice which requires all round abilities and skills will increase and the intellectual challenge presented will be significant. New knowledge will have to be acquired and applied, in association with traditional capabilities, in novel ways. The principal new knowledge required will be an understanding of information technology and an up-to-date knowledge of its potential. Costing and justification of projects will become a more vital consideration. The ability to secure change effectively will be more important than ever.

2 Dimensions of importance in promoting the best use of information technology

During the course of an assignment it may be necessary to assess what might be gained from the application of information technology. Issues need to be examined under several heads. The four discussed below will all influence decisions but in differing degrees. The weight to be attached to each will vary according to individual circumstances, and the rate and nature of technological change. If potential applications are investigated in this way a reliable indication of what is best to do should be obtained. A further consideration to make in the appraisal of potential applications is whether they should be developed by the user with internal help, or by consultants. In the latter event the need for internal support can still be substantial and should not be underestimated.

3 Dimension I: Impact on how work is done

Many improvements aimed at better communication in administrative work will become possible during the next decade. There will be potential to reduce the degree of specialisation in some junior posts, and the demand for such posts will undergo change. Higher level posts will have the opportunity to become involved with document and data preparation. The need for some middle level management or specialist posts will have to be reviewed to ensure they are continuing to add a necessary contribution to the total effort. These developments will arise from the linkage of machines in new ways, the ability to access common data bases, and obtain a local processing capacity. The exact patterns that these developments will take are uncertain, and will in any case be much affected by local considerations. Many organisations will be involved, including trade unions and they will all need to be consulted.

Most of the innovations outlined above are dependent on the extended use of microcomputers and computer terminals. In combination they should allow additional spin-off benefits to occur, particularly structural reorganisation and changes in working practices. Wider gains in operating effectiveness should emerge, especially if management as a whole uses the improved information available to it to make better informed decisions, and individual managers improve their own working information systems.

Although information technology has considerable potential to increase efficiency in the way work is done, there are attendant costs and problems that have to be taken into account if a realistic appraisal of benefits is to be made. Much training will be required if the capabilities of the technology are to be anywhere near fully maximised. Care must be taken to assess the claims for equipment capability made by manufacturers, especially those relating to the availability of operational facilities. There is danger too that capital and staff effort will be wasted on inessential projects. Assignment staff should only be involved where the gains are likely to be significant and minor applications should be dealt with by local management.

4 Dimension II: Availability and cost of equipment

The following usage patterns will be basic alternatives, depending on inter-relationship of efficiency and cost factors. The first is general availability, as typified by the distribution of the telephone in modern offices, and the second is limited availability in concentrated units so that efficiency is maximised, as in the use of the typing pool. Pilot schemes and experiments between manufacturers and potential users are often undertaken to seek and clarify understanding of what is possible. These are very helpful to assignment staff for they provide up-to-date information about practical developments. Direct association with experiments of this kind enables valuable background knowledge to be gained, which can be used when advising others. The viability of specific applications of information technology will obviously be much affected by trends in costs, the future pattern of which are, unfortunately, not clear. While in the longer term equipment costs will most likely decline, expenditure on staff involved in systems design and software production will probably increase. Criteria should be defined for controlling applications if possible and these should take account of variations in the cost elements involved.

5 Dimension III: Impact on management operations and structures

In policy areas the 'team' approach to the completion of work will still be necessary, but staff should be able to control the preparation of papers directly, and operate at a higher work rate through the personal use of word processors. There will be potential for increased efficiency as a result of this, allied with a reduction in the need for support services. The wider availability of equipment and standard programmes can lead to a much greater use of statistical and operational research techniques in policy formulation, but care needs to be taken to establish their relevance in any particular situation.

In executive areas senior management should require less support in monitoring and controlling aspects of their work, and opportunities may occur to shorten the management chain or remove specialist posts. The extent that this will be possible is unclear since management may turn its attention to other tasks, eg more effective supervision. Traditional duties may be replaced with newly emerged ones, for example the co-ordination of the information technology system itself. It should be possible to give greater attention to planning, co-ordination and control because of improvements in the content and flow of management information.

As information technology is progressively applied there will be opportunities for management to work across traditional boundaries. New organisation structures and combinations of roles will be possible leading to rationalisation, increases in effectiveness, and possible staff savings. These types of developments may well be potentially the most productive to emerge from the increased application of information technology; they will however tend not to develop naturally since there is a good deal of inertia in organisations. Assignment staff should always be on the look out to obtain the widest possible benefits from individual applications. This will only be achieved if close attention is given to the 'macro' level when investigations of organisations are made.

More than ever central functions in organisations will require information to be readily available if they are to play an effective co-ordinating role. This will be essential if individual units within the organisation, possibly operating on a highly decentralised basis, are to retain an overall compatibility with each other.

6 Dimension IV: Obstacles to acceptance of change

This aspect of assignment work has been given prominence elsewhere in the book. Yet experience teaches that many problems arise in the application of information technology because gaining acceptance of new ways of working is not given sufficient consideration. In fact special attention should be focused on this matter in such projects, as there is often a large amount of change involved.

Full and open consultation with staff and staff representatives is essential at all stages, particularly in relation to the impact on job content, responsibilities, and job security. Where major change is involved considerable effort needs to be allocated to planning the achievement of change and to communication and training in new techniques. System requirements must be carefully identified in close consultation with the user, and care taken to ensure that the equipment supplied, including the conditions of supply, is satisfactory.

7 The importance of planning and appraisal in implementing projects

Because individual information technology applications will only be made to meet the needs of local situations they will vary considerably in structure and design, and the greater the sophistication of equipment becomes, the more true will this be. Assignment staff will not be able to provide effective advice unless they understand fully both the local work situation, and how best to use information technology. These factors highlight how essential effective project appraisal will be in the future, particularly as line management takes more responsibility for individual projects. Potential applications must never be accepted at face value, and it is necessary for assignment staff to evaluate critically:

- manufacturer's estimates for their equipment;
- line management's estimates of their essential requirements;
- the preliminary costing of the application, which is often prepared by local management.

There are a number of basic questions that always have to be asked about the viability of a project. These should be considered early in the planning stage, and repeated again before final decisions are made to go ahead.

- In terms of long and short timescales (more than or less than two years) is the investment worthwhile?

    Is the project meeting the real need of the situation? (long term)

    Does the project facilitate or enable adaptation as operating experience is gained? (long term)

    What is the relative priority of the project compared with others? (long term)

    Is the project really suitable for computerisation? (short and long term, depending on the context)

    Will the project provoke 'man-machine' interface problems? (short term)

- Is the best use being made of the currently available technology? Will it be possible to make technical improvements without incurring prohibitive costs?

- If the approach decided upon is a piecemeal one, is it consciously based on sound judgement that this is the best that can be done in the circumstances?
- Is there a need to link up with other potential applications? What are the implications for the viability of this particular project?

As well as being tested from the point of view of need, overall viability, and technical suitability all projects must be justified, ie examined to see if they actually produce savings, and are necessary. The user's part in this, in view of how projects are likely to originate increasingly in the future, is very important. Proposals put forward by the user should be thoroughly assessed. It is easy to embark on a computer-related project which does not, in the end, produce the savings or gains claimed. Unless there are clear overriding policy considerations no project should go ahead if it cannot be justified on this basis. Project benefits should be carefully defined and costed.

A cost benefit analysis should be prepared, and a project justification exercise completed, ie advantages and disadvantages should be weighed against other alternatives. Cost and benefit options should be expressed in financial terms whenever possible. When these appraisals are made it is important the following factors are not overlooked:

- the degree of technical risk involved;
- additional staff costs;
- effort required in the installation of the new system;
- changes in need that are likely to arise as operational experience is gained;
- costs involved in running the new and old systems in tandem.

Once confirmed the project must be adequately planned through all its stages, and adequate provision made for the various kinds of consultation that may be required. Planning for change should be included, and adequate provision made to cover such matters as job satisfaction, job definition and grading.

CHAPTER X: IMPROVING THE USE OF RESOURCES

1 Meeting the changing needs of management

The task of the assignment officer is always to help line management meet its responsibilities more effectively and efficiently, but the ways in which this is achieved are continually developing. Various influences can prompt new approaches. Some are technologically based, as is clear from the previous chapter on the impact of information technology. Changes in management practice can also have an impact, and alterations of this kind are now in progress that will affect assignment work in the future.

Line management in the Civil Service is becoming directly accountable for more aspects of resource management. How this development will influence assignment work in the future will obviously depend on the type of work performed by line management and the environment which prevails. The impact is likely to be very variable in character, and develop gradually, so assignment staff should be able to meet the need as it arises. But they must be aware of the developments occurring and be ready to respond when required to do so. This is particularly true in two types of situation. If an assignment is to be conducted in an area where management is constrained tightly by financial budgets and objectives, it is clearly vital that the assignment officer understands and relates to the needs of the situation in making proposals. It is equally important that those who have been asked to improve efficiency in areas not so tightly constrained, should know enough about budget and objective setting techniques to be able to apply them as necessary.

Many methods can be applied to monitor and improve the use of resources, and where management's accountability and responsibility are being increased one of the more important is the budgetary system. This practice is not new to the Civil Service, but it is likely it will come to feature more generally and prominently as an aid to management than has been the case in the past. Even if assignment staff are not involved in the initiation of budgets and budgetary systems, they can play an important advisory role in helping management to operate their budgetary responsibilities efficiently and effectively. Management is clearly going to need specialist help, particularly where the work is complex.

2 The management services contribution

Advice on the operation of budgetary systems is likely to grow and the types of issues most likely to arise are outlined below. Some can overlap with each other.

- Problems in controlling the budget because of poor or inappropriate division of responsibility in a department, or segment of a department.
- Need to improve 'loose' or 'tight' budgets arising from inadequate assessment of the workload and the resources required to complete it.
- Need to redefine information systems, working procedures, organisational arrangements etc where poor definition is inhibiting the effective operation of budgetary responsibilities.
- Need to improve definition of objectives and performance indicators because they are either inappropriate or poorly expressed.

In the course of assignment work in areas where budgetary systems are only partly applied, or are absent, assignment staff should be concerned to find out whether such systems could be introduced. Appropriate recommendations should be put forward to introduce budgetary systems, which should include at least an outline of the type of systems that would be most suitable.

As well as responding to management's needs in regard to the operation of budgets, assignment staff should take the initiative in furthering the best general use of resources whenever possible. There will be particular opportunity for this where overall cash budgets are applied. Assignments should include assessment of how resources are deployed, with a view to maximising their use in support of the main task. There are various ways in which the issue can be pursued. Ensuring that work is computerised only if the development is justified is one example, and another is to actually check that the bulk of resources are actively deployed on the most important tasks.

These requirements will present a challenge to management services. Although learning a completely new discipline will not be necessary, traditional skills will have to be developed in new ways, new techniques used, and the familiar ones applied in more extensive ways. It is also likely that traditional working practices will be modified, both in the conduct of assignments and through the increased joint working of the various management services disciplines.

Assignments which arise from managers' perceived needs to meet their budgetary responsibilities will tend to be rather less specific in character than the traditional type. This will be true, whether they occur in support of top management in its task of maintaining the overall strategy, or at the request of individual managers. There will be at least one major reason for the lack of specific direction. When managers have an overall problem in meeting their budgets they will tend to seek general guidance on how to resolve it rather than ask for specific advice. This will be so because of the number of separate elements within a budget, ie staff, accommodation, equipment, support costs, and the overall complexity of the interrelationship of these with the organisation structure and objectives set. Managers are likely to be aware of the existence of a problem, but be unable to identify exactly what it is. In such circumstances more emphasis will need to be placed on investigation of overall effectiveness within areas of responsibility, than on the improvement of specific administrative functions or procedures.

To illustrate such developments four types of potential problems that can arise in the operation of budgetary systems are set out below, together with an indication of the management services contribution to their resolution. All these problems could initially be presented as inability to meet budgetary requirements.

- *Example problem: objective setting and monitoring.* Managers have unclear objectives.

  Management services contribution. Is objective setting, and the creation of appropriate operating structures and systems taking place effectively at top management levels? Are these decisions communicated meaningfully to people at lower levels? Are the overall objectives of the department being met? Are the objectives defined capable of being met? Help may be provided in defining objectives and performance indicators.

- *Example problem: definition of responsibilities.* Managers do not have clearly defined responsibilities within which to operate, and feel they are artificially constrained.

  Management services contribution. Are departmental structures and operating systems designed so that it is possible to define responsibilities clearly, and fairly make people accountable? How could the arrangements be modified to allow managers to operate more freely within clearly defined parameters? Help may be provided in the improvement of organisation structure, job definition, information flows and procedure definition.

- *Example problem: availability of information.* Information for line management, including costs, performance achievements, personal training and available advice, appear to be inadequate to meet objectives and responsibilities.

  Management services contribution. Are the information systems appropriate? Do they fit with the organisation? Are the information systems clearly defined for the tasks to be completed? Is all the information required available to assess output, staff activity and costs? Are objectives and performance indicators defined appropriately? Is the organisation's structure designed correctly? Help may be given to establish information and training needs for all the posts involved, in the definition of procedures by which information is made available, and also as to how the information may be provided most efficiently.

- *Example problem: general inability to meet budgetary requirements.* Management is confused and unclear about how to improve its performance or meet its budgetary requirements.

  Management services contribution. When this situation exists, and there is no clear lead as to the cause of the problem an overall investigation of the organisation is essential. It may be difficult to get at the real cause, because of the interrelationship of the separate elements which exist in the budget responsibility. The following types of questions should be asked. Is the overall operating system, including structure and systems, appropriate? Is the organisation structured so as to allow achievable objectives to be met and performance indicators devised? Is management being given information at the right level of detail? Is the budget realistic in relation to the workload and the resources available? Advice may be given to improve the overall structure of the organisation, to ensure that information systems and procedures support the structure and to define jobs clearly. Help may also be given towards setting objectives and to the identification of performance indicators for the redesigned organisation.

3 Important techniques

Some of the techniques which are required to solve the types of problems outlined above are ones that assignment staff have not traditionally been familiar with; others are better known but will require adaptation to the new circumstances. A few of the more important techniques likely to be used are listed below.

Costing of activities. The collection of ongoing costs of activities, particularly of administrative work, is an application of the costing technique which has a number of important uses in the Civil Service. It is a means for determining exactly how money has been spent on a service or activity, either overall, or broken down by component parts. Costing of this type can provide the basic information for budget creation, particularly if it is available historically over a period of several years, and it is also of use in making predictions of future costs. Regularly collected information on costs can additionally provide a standard against which to measure performance, and is a powerful diagnostic tool for assignment staff.

Budgeting. The preparation of realistic budgets is not an easy task, and requires not only the careful projection of cost information, but also the collection of cost data in ways which will effectively support budget formulation. Operating problems will inevitably arise that will require the basis on which budgets have been drawn up to be reassessed. Effective budget operation is also dependent on organisation structures and information systems being so arranged that they support budget operation. The degree to which necessary resources are available also affects budget operation. All these matters are of concern to assignment staff when involved in the investigation of budget operating problems.

The identification and monitoring of objectives and performance indicators. The successful application of these techniques has provide for clear objectives and suitable performance indicators to be established; and, secondly, the techniques themselves must be sensibly applied to the immediate working context. Assignment staff need to be knowledgeable about how to set objectives and monitor performance, and be able to provide advice on these matters.

Organisation analysis. This will become more important for two reasons. Problems in the fulfilment of budgetary responsibilities may originate from ill-defined division of work within the overall organisational unit, and from poor definition of operational systems. Weaknesses of this type prevent budgets and objectives from being established clearly. Secondly, the origin of problems may be hidden within the interrelationship of constituent parts of the budget. In such circumstances it will be necessary to analyse all, or at least a number of aspects, of the budget's structure and its organisational setting in order to identify exactly what is wrong.

Work measurement. Manpower is a very large component in Civil Service budgets. This technique has an important place in helping to determine the amount of manpower resource required to complete a known workload. It is also of use in the determination of quantitative performance indicators. Assignment staff will find this technique of value in investigating staff levels and performance indicators to see if they are correctly determined and applied.

GLOSSARY

In drawing up this glossary, reference has been made to the British Standard Glossary of Terms Used in Work Study and Organisation and Methods (O&M) BS 3138: 1979.

ACTION PLAN   A plan included in an assignment report which is agreed between the assignment officer and client, which identifies the responsibilities of each for the implementation of proposals, and the timescales to be allowed.

ASSIGNMENT   A specific investigation of a stated problem or issue together with the identification of practical proposals for change, usually in the form of a written report. An assignment most often occurs by request and can be completed by an individual or a team. The term project has a very similar meaning.

ASSIGNMENT MANAGER   Team leader responsible for control of the allocation of resources allowed for the completion of an assignment, and for monitoring the completion of the work. The term project leader is very similar in meaning, although the responsibility for resources may be more constrained and have more emphasis on team leadership.

ASSIGNMENT OFFICER   The individual who completes the detailed work of an assignment. One or two other words are used in the text, the meanings of which are very similar, eg specialist and management services adviser.

ASSIGNMENT STAFF   A generic term for all those professionally involved in an assignment, who may be assignment officers or the assignment manager.

AUDIT   See scrutiny.

CLIENT	The individual who requests an assignment and for whom it is completed. The term multiple clients is used to indicate that some assignments have more than one client. Sometimes the client is not the original source of the assignment but a spokesman working on behalf of a sponsor (see individual entry).
COMPLETION PLAN	A plan for the conduct of an assignment which is drawn up before it starts, and includes the contract (terms of reference, resources required, time allowed and roles of parties), the individual stages and their work contents, and progress review points.
CUSTOMER	The individual for whom the assignment is completed. The client figures prominently in this respect but is not necessarily the only party to be treated as such. People who use the system must also have their interests taken into account.
CYCLIC REVIEW	The regular examination of work or procedures, so that an organisational entity is wholly examined within a stated period of time.
DATA	Raw facts.
INFORMATION	Data which either directly, or after analysis, can be used practically.
INFORMATION TECHNOLOGY	The acquisition, processing, storage, dissemination, and use of vocal, pictorial, textual and numerical information by a micro-electronics based combination of computer and telecommunications.
INTERNAL AUDIT	An independent appraisal activity within an organisation for the review of accounting, financial and other operations as a basis for service to management. It is a managerial control which functions by managing and evaluating the effectiveness of other controls.
LINE MANAGER	A manager whose responsibilities lie within the completion of an organisation's main function. The term is also used in various modified ways to denote differences in hierarchical position within line management, eg top management, senior management, operational management, local line management. The terms do not identify precise grades in the hierarchy but relative position and role in whatever situation may arise. See also individual entries.

LOCAL LINE MANAGER	The responsible manager in an operational hierarchy which has wider equivalents, eg regional or national. See line manager.
MANAGEMENT SERVICES	Specialist groups or units established within organisations to assist and advise on improvements in executive management functions.
MANAGEMENT SERVICES ADVISER	See assignment officer.
MANAGEMENT SERVICES STAFF	Personnel working at any level within the internal consultancy service.
MODEL FRAMEWORK	A statement of principles which sets out suggested practice in an ideal way, for use as a guide in practical work.
MULTI-DISCIPLINARY TEAM	The working together, under a single manager, of assignment officers from several management services disciplines, eg organisation and methods, staff inspection, operational research.
OPERATIONAL MANAGEMENT	Management responsible for implementation of agreed policy. See line manager.
ORGANISATION AND METHODS (O&M)	The systematic study of the structure of an organisation, its management, control, procedures and methods, undertaken to increase its efficiency.
PROJECT	The term is interchangeable with assignment, see individual entry.
PROJECT LEADER	See assignment manager.
PROPOSALS	Detailed and specific suggestions to improve working arrangements, expressed verbally or in writing.
RECOMMENDATIONS	See proposals. The two words are used interchangeably.
REVIEW	See scrutiny.
SCRUTINY	An assignment which is decided upon by central or top management. The term is often applied to an investigation of wide significance for a department or the whole of the Civil Service. The terms audit and review have a similar meaning, although audit is sometimes associated with work completed on a regular and cyclic basis.
SENIOR MANAGEMENT	Management which has significant executive authority. See line manager.

SKILL	In management services terms the ability to complete an assignment effectively. It is the product of understanding, the effective use of techniques and judgement, and the overall application of these to a particular situation. Skill is also proficiency in a particular technique.
SPECIALIST	See assignment officer.
SPONSOR	The individual who is the prime mover behind an assignment and who does not necessarily act as a major spokesman on its behalf with assignment staff.
STAFF INSPECTION	Staff inspection is a formal check on the planning, allocation and use of manpower resources. It examines specifically: need for work, organisation structure, numbers of people required and grading standards.
SURVEY	Similar to an assignment, but usually more general in scope, eg the study of a procedure or service across a department. See scrutiny and assignment.
TOP MANAGEMENT	Management with the highest level of freedom to decide. See line manager.
VALUE ADDED	The material and real gain obtained by the organisation from proposals arising from an assignment, which should be precise even if they are not capable of being quantified.

INDEX

Agreement 61–63
Analysis 35–44
    models 40–44
Assignment staff
    impartiality 13
    interpersonal skills 21, 23
    modus operandi 14–15
    role 12–15
    role in implementing
    proposals 72–74
Assignments
    and change 20–24
    contract 22–23
    management of 15–17
    objectives of 9, 13, 22, 32, 87–88
    planning 15, 19–20, 24–27
    relationship to wider context 19
    sequence of action 25, 29–33
    stages of assignment 29–32
    terms of reference 30, 32
    types of assignment 15

Change 19–24
    acceptance of change 23–24, 80–81
    and information technology 80–81
    planning for 20–21, 23, 72–73
Charting 40, 55–56
Completion plan 24–27
Computers
    use in storing and analysing data 40, 50, 56
Consultation 14, 23
Contract 22–23, 32–33
Cost analysis 44, 54, 87
Costing systems 52–54
Creative thinking 56–57

Data
    analysis 35–36, 41–43
    collection 37–40, 45–49
    evaluation 39–40, 49–51
    organisation of 39–40
    usage 35
Diagnosis 43–44

Entry stage 29–32

Forms design 54

Implementation 14–15, 24, 71–74
Information technology 75–82
    applications of 77–78
    and change 80–81
    hardware 74–80
    impact on jobs 76, 78–79
    impact on management 79–80
    introduction of 75–76
Initial contacts 30
Interviewing 39, 45–49

Line management 83–87
    accountability 15–17
    and implementation of proposals 12, 61–62, 71–72
    role 11–12

Management *see* Line management, Senior management
Management services 84–87
Models for analysis 40–44
Monitoring 26–27, 32

Open approach 21
Operational research 55
Organisation charts *see* Charting

93

Participative approach 19–20
Preliminary survey 30–31
Project network technique 55
Proposals
    agreement on 61–63
    formulation 59–61

Questionnaires 39

Recommendations *see* Proposals
Reports
    presentation of reports 65–70
    verbal reports 68–70
    written reports 65–68
Resources 32, 83–85, 87

Sampling 39
Senior management involvement 33
Specialists *see* Assignment staff
Statistical analysis 40, 49–52

Time allocated 32
Training 73–74

Verbal reports 68–70

Work measurement 52, 88
Written reports 65–68